GAME 1

THOMAS H. PAULY

GAME
FACES

Five Early American Champions
and the Sports They Changed

University of Nebraska Press　Lincoln & London

A different version of chapter 1 originally appeared
in *Around the World on a Bicycle* by Thomas Stevens
(Mechanicsburg pa: Stackpole Books, 2001).
Portions of chapter 3 originally appeared as
"A Man for Two Seasons: Bill Reid Jr.,"
Harvard Magazine (Nov.–Dec. 1991): 67–72.

Library of Congress Cataloging-in-Publication Data
Pauly, Thomas H.
Game faces: five early American champions
and the sports they changed / Thomas H. Pauly.
p. cm.
Includes bibliographical references and index.
isbn 978-0-8032-3817-6 (pbk.: alk. paper)
1. Athletes—United States—Biography.
2. Sports—United States—History—19th century.
3. Sports—United States—History—
20th century. I. Title.
GV697.A1P353 2012
796.0922—dc23
[B]
2011035847

Frontispiece, from the top: Tom Stevens,
Fanny Bullock Workman, Bill Reid,
May Sutton, and Barney Oldfield.
These photographs are reproduced
in their entirety in the interior.

Set in Sabon by Bob Reitz.

For my wife, Suzanne, whose cheerfulness, lively conversation, and wonderful meals have kept me going.

Contents

Introduction

People today think of the early days of American sport in terms of the 1920s. This is not to say that they believe sports originated during this period, but rather they remember its champions: Babe Ruth, Red Grange, Helen Wills, and Bobby Jones. Each competed in a sport popular then and even more so now. The enduring fame of these athletes is, of course, rooted in their remarkable accomplishments, but it is equally indebted to a culture that aggrandized those accomplishments.

Jay Gatsby's "old sport" greeting of an acquaintance, dated though it sounds, attests to the widespread interest in sport at the time. Powerful commercial forces were stoking this interest and focusing national attention on athletes who excelled. Newspapers were the single most influential factor. By 1925 one-quarter of all newspapers sold were purchased for their sports pages.[1] In 1919 400 journalists and 20,000 spectators attended the fight between Jess Willard and Jack Dempsey.[2] Seven years later, at Dempsey's first match against Gene Tunney, these numbers soared to 1,800 correspondents and 130,000 spectators.[3] When Bobby Jones successfully achieved the fourth victory of the first Grand Slam, sportswriters cranked out an estimated two million words of coverage.[4]

Sales of radios, which only began with the opening of the first transmitting station in 1920, soared to the point that 40 percent of all households had one by the decade's end. As the popularity of live reports of sporting events outstripped transmission capability, resourceful announcers learned to improvise eye-witness narratives from wired information. These "reporters" in distant station booths, like those actually at the event, skillfully cued the tenor of their voices to the emotion of the moment and accentuated the successes or disappointments of favorites. The blare of tabloids, another newcomer from 1919, intensified pressure on established newspapers to hire a new breed of sportswriter adept at personalizing athletes and enlivening their performances. Grantland Rice wrote himself into history with the famous opening of his *New York Herald Tribune* account of Notre Dame's 1924 victory over Army: "Outlined against a blue-gray sky the Four Horsemen rode again. In dramatic lore they are known as famine, pestilence, destruction and death. These are only aliases. Their real names are: Stuhldreher, Miller, Crowley and Layden." Along with Ring Lardner, Damon Runyon, Westbrook Pegler, and Heywood Broun, he transformed accomplished athletes into legendary ones. Their presentation conceded immediacy to newscasters and crafted absorbing accounts that sold newspapers to readers already aware of the final score. They inspired a proliferation of sobriquets—"the Sultan of Swat," "the Galloping Ghost," "Little Miss Poker Face," and "the Manassa Mauler," which aided in fashioning heroes who were simultaneously awesome *and* familiar.

Sports reporters encouraged ordinary citizens to believe that they knew and understood their champions. Older

defenders of journalistic accuracy and respectability objected to this contrivance and perceived younger reporters as
seeking the same fame and fortune that athletes enjoyed.[5]
"Present-day opinion of newspaper editors, psychologists,
trades publication editors, advertising men, and journalism
instructors is that sports on their present scale would be
impossible without the sports section of the daily papers,"
reported *Editor and Publisher* in 1927. "Without the assis-
tance of the newspapers, sports would never have attained
their present popularity."[6] In short, we remember the champions of the 1920s because newspapers, radios, and newsreels so effectively branded them on the consciousness of our
culture.

The figures in this book date from an earlier era when
sports were still developing and beginning to attract this
kind of notice. Except for automobile racing, the sports represented here—bicycling, football, tennis, and mountaineering—originated during the aftermath of the Civil War and
were powerfully influenced by the surge in industrialization
and commercialization that war unleashed. To hard-working
middle-class Americans, these two developments increased
the appeal of recreation and sport as meaningful alternatives.
Prior to the Civil War, as the country converted from Cal-
vinism to capitalism, responsible citizens believed that they
had to work hard and save. Industry, productivity, and perseverance determined the success of the individual and the
nation. Leisure and idleness, on the other hand, were vices
fraught with moral, financial, and political hazard. However,
the new and enlarged middle class that emerged following
the Civil War had the capital and the incentive to question
and then amend the puritanical values they inherited. Still

believing work to be necessary and gainful, these ambitious, upwardly mobile citizens began to sense that working conditions had grown claustrophobic, regimented, and debilitating. Was it not better, they reasoned, to spend time away from the factory or office and use recreation and vacation to counteract these damaging effects? Paradoxically, the various new games they embraced as escape rapidly came to be seen as effective therapy that would rehabilitate players into more productive workers. Moreover, the informality and relaxation that made sport such a valued alternative developed its own set of expectations, organizations, and regulations and functioned as a meaningful complement to the workplace.

Differentiated at first by the physical activity each involved, sports appealed to citizens as play for adults, and participation was judged to be more important than competition and victory. The high-wheel bicycle, which appeared following the 1876 Centennial Exposition, was promoted as healthy exercise and a stimulus for cordiality, but manufacturers strongly discouraged racing. Nevertheless, competition proved impossible to marginalize or suppress in the ensuing expansion of sport. Meanwhile, people naturally gravitated to individuals and teams that excelled, and many discovered that they preferred to be spectators rather than participants. Initially, small numbers of supporters and enthusiasts gathered along the boundaries of play, but they soon swelled into restless crowds hoping for better accommodation and improved performance. Resourceful entrepreneurs sprang up to address these expectations. In return for admission fees, they arranged schedules and seating and raised financing for the costs of equipment and travel. These responsibilities fostered exchange and led to the formation of cooperative organizations and standardized rules for events.

During the 1880s, as newspapers noticed reader interest in the proliferating contests, they started offering final scores and abbreviated summaries of the action. Two telling measures of the growth of this interest were the expanding length of these accounts and their transition from bits of news randomly inserted into features and their eventual consolidation into a designated section for sports. By the 1890s every major newspaper had at least one reporter concentrating on sport, and magazines began to concentrate on a single sport.[7] *American Lawn Tennis* (1898) and *Golf* (1900) offered expensive oversized formats and slick paper for their upscale readership. Fifteen years before, *Outing* was so far ahead of this trend that the magazine incurred a substantial loss when it was resold two years after its purchase. The new editor's decision to enlarge its focus and cover more competitions developed it into the leading journal of sport, but it did not become profitable until 1895, when its circulation reached ninety thousand.[8]

The sporting goods business furnishes an equally vivid measure of this growth. During the 1870s manufacturers of wood, leather, and textile products noticed sport as an area of promise, and by 1880 eighty were offering some kind of gear. The first retail outlets for this merchandise targeted baseball enthusiasts, then the largest market, and the most successful of these was the A. G. Spalding Company, which opened in Chicago in 1876, a year after Spalding arrived to be captain and manager of the Chicago White Stockings. As support for this venture, he brought out a booklet titled *Spalding's Official Baseball Guide*, secured a contract from the National League for official baseballs and bats, and quickly became the largest purveyor of baseball equipment. When his annual baseball guide achieved a circulation of fifty thousand in 1885, he acquired the American Publishing Company and commenced a line of *Official Guides* for other sports, each addition affirming that the sport being covered had enough participants and enthusiasts to be a viable market. He bolstered this diversification with acquisition of manufacturers of bicycles and tennis equipment and establishment of thirteen more retail outlets in other cities. By 1900 Spalding was the dominant merchant, but business was so strong that there were now 144 manufacturers of sporting goods, including the recently founded Rawlings (1888) and Abercrombie and Fitch (1900), both of which attained instant success.[9]

The five champions profiled in this book date from this earlier period, predating the 1920s and World War I, when sporting events were first commercialized and achieved popularity. Although few today recognize the names of Tom Stevens, Fanny Bullock Workman, Bill Reid, May Sutton, or Barney Oldfield, each was a stellar performer and famous at the time. Stevens was the first man to ride a bicycle, "a high wheeler," around the world (1884–87). Workman, accompanied by her husband, completed seven expeditions into the Himalayas between 1898 and 1912 and was among the first three climbers to reach an elevation of 23,000 feet, a feat that was not surpassed by another woman until thirty years later. Bill Reid was one of Harvard's greatest athletes and following his graduation, coached its football team through three glorious seasons, but his greatest accomplishment was his role in saving the game from a national movement for its abolition in 1905. Sutton, a tennis player from California, was the youngest winner of singles at the 1904

National Championships (now the U.S. Open) until Tracy Austin (1979) and the first American woman to triumph at Wimbledon (1905). Oldfield was the first champion of motorcar racing and so resourceful at capitalizing on his success that he almost destroyed the sport.

Although these male and female champions are usually mentioned in histories of their sports, remarkably little has been written about them and their careers. Currently the only book devoted to any of them is a fifty-year-old biography of Barney Oldfield by an author who was more an enthusiast than a scholar. When I started this project, I was hoping to turn up a prominent athlete from the past who warranted fresh research and legitimately deserved to be better known. In my previous publications, I had already gravitated toward similarly neglected achievers from literature and the theater. My initial research yielded enough possibilities that choosing one became difficult, and I concluded that a selection of profiles might be a refreshing alternative to the conventional biography. An equally important factor in my eventual choices was the colorful stories that lurked within the material I was finding. I did not want tales that smacked of contrivance, like those of the titans and folk heroes promoted by sportswriters since the 1920s. Certainly the period I was researching contained many forgotten champions who dominated races, clobbered opponents, and amassed victories. I wanted both something else and something more. I preferred the warts—the eccentricities, the self-righteousness, and the prejudices—that made my choices both successful and offensive. I was even more interested in the intense drive of all five to excel and triumph and their shared belief that sport should be more than play.

Nonetheless, far and away the most important factor in my eventual choices was what their careers revealed about the ongoing transformation of sport from casual recreation into commercialized contests involving accomplished players and close supervision. The title I have chosen for this book, *Game Faces*, is meant to signal my dual intent of presenting these biographical profiles as portraits of their sports as well. In both respects, they are faces of change. The sports that initially attracted these champions were quite different from the ones we know, but the years of their participation evolved a much closer approximation. Although various issues contributed to this change, three stand out in the chapters ahead and function as themes that link and interconnect them.[10]

Of the three, money is the most important. The often-heard complaint today that sport has been corrupted by money echoes from the dawn of sport and ignores the hard fact that money has always been essential to sport. Sites, equipment, travel, and accommodations cost money, and once locals outgrew the attraction of playing one another on a nearby field, they needed funding. This problem was complicated by the fact that nineteenth-century culture, so intent on turning a profit in the workplace, believed that sport should be for amateurs and that monetary gain was a menace.

Unsurprisingly, the strongest supporters of this thinking were the wealthy, who had the leisure and means for sport. Although the concept of amateurism is usually traced to the London Athletic Club in England (1863), it was first circulated in the United States by the New York Athletic Club (1866). In 1876 the NYAC mandated that its competitions be restricted to "any person who has never competed . . . for public or admission money . . . or taught or assisted in the pursuit of athletic exercises as a means of livelihood." Three years later the newly established National Association of Amateur Athletes of America espoused this definition of amateurism and won agreement from colleges and other clubs, like the New York Athletic Club, that were springing up around the country. Sport was most important to these organizations and clubs as a shared interest and stimulus for affiliation. Acceptance into an elite club or college conferred preeminent status and distinguished the recipient from the rest of society. Consciously this membership emulated upper-class English interests and activities, and less consciously they advocated amateurism because it favored people like themselves, who could afford sport, and excluded those from down the social scale who could not. This thinking was personified in the so-called gentleman amateur, who vigorously opposed athletic games for money and was cavalier about rules.[11]

However, the same money that initially empowered the diverse versions of this figure in the pages ahead quickly turned against them and undermined their authority and privilege. American sport had too much appeal to be confined within upper-class preserves. The allure of financial gain unleashed the democratizing power of capitalism. In order to sell more goods, more newspapers, and more tickets, agents of commerce curried and stoked the attention of the middle class and below. Demands for greater competition and more victories from enthusiasts inspired these merchants to deploy their profits as investment. They cautiously backed competitions that accommodated an enlarged range of participants. Justifiably wary of the deep-seated commitment to amateurism and widespread suspicion of professionalism, they conspired to expand and exploit gray areas in these biases.

Rules and organizations would loom almost as large as money in this early transformation of sport. Initial enthusiasts quickly grasped the importance of regulations to their games. First and foremost were the issues of how the new sport should be played and then which actions should be allowed and which ones should not. The "gentleman amateur," who influenced these basics, favored casual associations and lax rules; he embraced sport as an escape from obligation and restriction. When this freedom spawned problems, as it inevitably did, he turned to his club affiliation to work out a better arrangement. This initial concession of his authority and independence was increased by those whose enthusiasm for a particular sport carried them to specialist organizations like the League of American Wheelmen, the Intercollegiate Football Association, and the American Automobile Association. These groups were more willing and better qualified to deliberate on behalf of their sports and to formulate new and better rules. Although social biases would remain a potent force within these organizations, some more so than others, their accomplishments inevitably diminished their receptivity to further changes. Some managed to rise above their biases and past, but those that did usually did so because outsiders and commercial forces pressured them.

Like water from a storm, the need for sport to broaden its range of participants, to enlarge its sources of funding, and to amend its existing rules produced a route over and around the obstacles in its path. In their quest for distinction and success, the champions in these chapters found themselves embroiled in upheaval and forced to reflect upon the acceptability of the existing rules of their sports—whether to abide by them or campaign for alternatives. The decisions of several were determined by whether they came from wealth. Others needed to seize upon an opening and turn it into opportunity. Some shifted from one position to the other. If each case has its own special configuration of these components, they collectively offer an illuminating portrait of how sport evolved during this period from recreational diversion into strenuous, regulated competition.

These chapters also feature pitched battles between their protagonists and archrivals. Since competition is the essence of sport—and increasingly so over this period—such contests are hardly surprising. The most enticing matches are usually ones in which a reigning champion confronts a contender with equivalent talent and a differing philosophy and style of play. Needless to say, the stakes involved can be very high, and they were especially so here. As money, rules, and mediating organizations intruded on these reckonings, the outcomes determined not only winners but also the future direction of their sports.

ONE

Tom Stevens

Bicycling and the Obstacle of Amateurism

On August 4, 1884, 104 days after his departure from San Francisco, Thomas Stevens reached Boston and completed the first bicycle trip across the United States. Eight months later he departed for England to extend his journey and finished his solo trip of two and a half years on January 8, 1887. To have ridden his "high wheeler" around the world and through regions where he was the first Westerner ever encountered—a mere fifteen years after Jules Verne *imagined* such a trip in various conveyances—was a remarkable feat. During an era of limited railroad service, when people in many areas of the world still relied on rough trails, animals, and wagons to make twenty miles a day, Stevens proved that his bicycle could average twice as much distance with less effort; under favorable conditions, he could outrun horses. He convinced skeptics from his own culture and less developed ones as well that the bicycle was worth riding and a major industrial achievement. As one newspaper account observed, "Doubters will begin to think that the capabilities of the bicycle are greater than they ever thought."[1]

Stevens's daring journey through some of the remotest, most challenging areas of the world occurred as bicycles were first becoming viable commercial products and being promoted as healthy exercise. Manufacturers wanted riders to think of bicycling as a participatory sport for amateurs in which the benefits of exertion, socializing, and adventure outweighed those of winning races and money. Such thinking greatly advanced the cause of sport during this seminal period in which recreation was attracting a broad range of participants and destabilizing traditional class distinctions. Both Fanny Workman and Barney Oldfield, who are discussed in later chapters, came from radically different social backgrounds, but both initiated their involvement with sport on bicycles, experiences that gained them prowess and yearning for distinction.

If this commitment of manufacturers to amateurism was shrewd promotion for their product, they soon compromised when they realized ways of doing so that would boost bicycle sales even more. Stevens embarked on his original crossing of the United States as an escape from dead-end jobs as a manual laborer. Perhaps the two most important decisions of this trip were his purchase of an expensive Columbia Standard bicycle made by the Pope Manufacturing Company and his inclusion of writing materials among his extremely restricted supplies. Stevens was hoping that Col. Albert Pope would be sufficiently impressed by his accomplishment to finance the next leg of his trip. However, Pope's resourceful marketing of his product included foundation of the League of American Wheelmen, whose rules prohibited all professionalism. Although Pope's sales strategy initially deprived Stevens of the kind of corporate sponsorship that is commonplace in sport today, the colonel did eventually fund him—but not for his trip, not for riding a Pope Columbia bicycle, and, above all, not directly. Pope belatedly agreed to pay Stevens as a correspondent for *Outing*, a magazine that he had recently purchased and enlarged to stimulate interest in outdoor sport, especially bicycling. Stevens's articles, which were later expanded into a book, were commissioned as validation for the wondrous potential of Pope's ungainly bicycle and his claims for all that a determined amateur might accomplish with it.[2]

The sketchy details of Stevens's life up to his departure evidence a restless quest for change and a better life. At twenty-nine, an age when most men are settled into their careers, Stevens decided his was going nowhere. Having worked for years in diverse menial jobs, he was ready for a radical departure that would satisfy his stifled yearning for opportunity and travel. Born in Great Berkhamstead in Hertfordshire, England, Stevens came from a background of poverty, hardship, and diminished prospects. Though he would claim that his ancestors were aristocrats and wealthy, he would also proudly insist that his immediate family was working class. He acquired his literacy from one of the rare English schools that provided free education, but dropped out early to become a grocer. His father's attempt at farming in Missouri so excited his own hopes that, when his father returned to England, Tom struck out on his own. After working on several Missouri ranches, he reconnected with his father and his family when they too immigrated and settled in nearby Clinton County. Sometime after 1878 he abandoned Missouri for the West and worked for two years in the rail mills of the Union Pacific in Laramie, Wyoming.[3] He then relocated to Colorado, where he tried mining until November 1883. At this point—*before he had ever been on a bicycle!*—he decided to ride one across the country.[4]

2. Thomas Stevens, 1878.

(Sam Perkins)

Stevens's discontent with his job caused him to notice the recent popularity of bicycles and perceive them as a potential escape from drudgery. Newspaper coverage of several failed attempts to ride across the country and new assaults being planned convinced him that acclaim and opportunity await-ed the first rider successfully to do so.[5] With no knowledge of bicycles beyond his understanding that manufacturers op-posed racing, he was confident that his familiarity with the mountains and deserts of the West more than compensated for his lack of riding experience. He perceived his opponent as the vast expanse of varied terrain to the east and the other riders aspiring to cross it first. Thus he pocketed his modest savings and struck out for San Francisco in the early spring of 1884. There he purchased a Columbia bicycle that had been shipped across the country from the Pope Manufactur-ing Company in Hartford, Connecticut. The astronomical $110 cost of this machine at the time is vividly illustrated by comparable prices for a tea set ($4.75), a sewing machine ($13.50), a set of parlor furniture ($17.50), and a 425-pound buggy ($44.50).[6] Although the reason for Stevens's invest-ment differed from that of most riders, it likewise represent-ed substantial trust in the reliability of his product.

Stevens's Standard Columbia was heavy (41 lbs.), uncom-fortable, and unstable. Modest uphill grades made riding impossible, while descents could be terrifying. His bicycle's mammoth front wheel, restricted steering, solid rubber tires, and crude brakes created a jolting ride and so destabilized the rider that he was in constant threat of a "header" and serious injury. Stevens was unable to ride more than three hundred miles without a header until he reached Europe (1:101).[7]

During his cross-country trip and especially in the far

more remote areas he later visited, Stevens was severely restricted in what he could carry. His supplies consisted of additional socks, an extra shirt, and an oiled cambric slicker that performed the multiple functions of raincoat, bedroll, and tent.[8] Necessity dictated that he drink water from along the way, no matter how suspect. Procurement of sustenance frequently superseded concern for quality and necessitated that he accept some truly suspect offerings like the bread in Khorāsān that was kneaded by hands covered with manure (2:83) and a vat of butter in China that contained strands of hair (1:403).

Bad food and water turned out to be lesser dangers. One of the most formidable challenges of Stevens's trip across the United States came within days of his early-spring departure when he chose to cross the Sierras on a railroad bed. Its mounded rock and ties compelled him to walk his bicycle much of the way, but unreliable schedules and the miles of shed protecting tracks from avalanches were an even greater problem. A train that caught Stevens in one of these sheds forced him to press himself and his bicycle against an adjacent mountainside and pray for adequate clearance. Another time one bore down on him midway across a high trestle, and he had to leap onto a narrow outcropping and dangle his bicycle over the gorge below (1:7, 16–9).

Near Fort Bridger, Wyoming, he got his first taste of truly hostile weather. A stretch of freezing rain spawned nine new streams. Most of these he crossed by using his bicycle as a vault, but twice he had to strip naked and ferry his possessions across. The second time the raging current was so menacing that he had to retrace his route. A freezing overnight in an abandoned wagon and portage of his bicycle for seven miles through a bone-chilling sea of mud pushed him to the brink of despair (1:58).[9] The remainder of the trip across the United States was demanding and taxing, but the roads, accommodations, and sources of support improved steadily.

The first part of his continuation, through England, Europe, and the Balkans, was surprisingly easy and uneventful, But once he moved beyond Tehran, following a winter layover there, the challenges resumed and became menacing. Again he started too early and was overtaken by spring snowstorms. The worst one left him floundering and desperate. After losing his grip on his bicycle during another stream crossing, he got drenched retrieving it and became truly hypothermic before finding a refuge (2:88–89). Later he almost drowned when he broke through the crusty bottom of another stream and was forced to swim both himself and his anchor-like bicycle to safety (2:126).

Crowds, which had hitherto been small and helpful, grew larger and threatening. As he progressed beyond the reach of railroads, his bicycle became *the* mechanized alternative to the horse and he a true wonder. His position atop the big wheel doubled his height, and its sparkling nickel frame communicated staggering wealth; Stevens was perceived as a deity, and word of his passing produced throngs to witness an exhibition of his riding. Whether he complied or pushed on, these massive gatherings quickly turned unruly and menacing (1:202–3, 362–63, 504–5; 2:69, 115–18). This threat became dire when he reached China and an indigenous xenophobia precipitated outright attacks. After a miraculous escape from a mob of stone throwers through the narrow streets of Ki-ngan-foo (2:418–23), Stevens hopped a boat and cut short his ride through China.

The worst moment of Stevens's entire trip involved no threat to his life. At the border of Afghanistan, long before he reached China, a customs official rejected his visa, which he had conscientiously procured months before, denied him entrance, and ruined his carefully laid plans. Although this setback saved him from *the* most dangerous country of his trip, one in which outsiders were routinely slain, he was forced to peddle back eight hundred miles to a port on the Caspian Sea, from which a series of steamers and trains took him back to Istanbul, through the Suez Canal, and on to Karachi.

Although these adversities sorely tested Stevens's courage and resourcefulness, another critical decision, one almost as important as the purchase of his Columbia Standard and his inclusion of writing supplies, was his belated decision to finish the initial leg of his trip in Boston, the corporate headquarters of the Pope Manufacturing Company. At the time Stevens acquired his Standard, Pope's company had been operating for less than seven years but was already producing 1,200 bicycles a year and reputed to be "the largest bicycle factory in the world."[10] Its owner, Col. Albert Pope, returned from the Civil War to become a manufacturer of gloves and shoes. By the 1870s he had achieved enough success to be seeking opportunities to expand and diversify. At the 1876 Centennial Exposition in Philadelphia, he first noticed some English high wheelers, "Penny-Farthings," but initially dismissed them as ungainly and impractical. "I remember my own impression as I gazed upon them," he remarked later, "wondering if it could be possible that any man, unless he were a skilled gymnast, could balance himself on one of them."[11] However, an Englishman named John Harrington

3. Col. Albert A. Pope.

alerted him to a superior machine, which he decided to import and sell. Customer feedback on defects carried him back to England to locate better parts, which he eventually assembled into his own bicycle. Next, he contracted space at the Weed Sewing Machine Company in Hartford and launched production.[12]

This new venture was immediately jeopardized by a lawsuit claiming that his machine infringed on a Lallement patent associated with the velocipede from years before. Rather than contest this claim, Pope purchased the patent. Shrewdly assessing the value of his components and their legal protection, he aggressively acquired their rights and vigilantly policed infringements.[13]

Marketing was as crucial to Pope's success as these patents. Because the high-wheel bicycle was both a weird contraption and a reminder of the disastrous velocipede, which riders characterized as a "bone-shaker," Pope had to overcome a mountain of buyer skepticism and resistance. As he once explained: "It was a great and hazardous undertaking to embark capital in the bicycle business when the public were so prejudiced against [it], remembering the total failure of the velocipede craze of earlier days. With one hand we had to create a demand, and with the other create the supply."[14]

One of the first things Pope did to spark interest and overcome market resistance was to start bicycle clubs. In 1878 he established the Massachusetts Bicycle Club with himself as president and family members in charge of its administration. A year later he created the Boston Bicycle Club for the local area and made his patent attorney Charles Pratt its president.[15] The following year he founded a national organization, the League of American Wheelmen (LAW), with

Pratt again as president, and located its headquarters in the same Boston building that housed Pope's corporate offices. While the main purpose of these organizations was to gather riders for fellowship, outings, and exchange of information, they also functioned as political forums for battling complaints against bicyclists and gaining them access to public roads. Thus the founding bylaws of the LAW defined as its mission "to promote the general interests of bicycling; to ascertain, defend, and protect the rights of wheelmen; and to encourage and facilitate touring."[16]

Crafty promotion accompanied establishment of these clubs. Pope encouraged Pratt's literary bent and paid the publishing costs for his *American Bicycler* (1879). Next, Pratt assembled a group of forty riders for a two-day, round-trip ride from Boston to Hartford and placed his account of it in the prestigious *Scribner's* magazine.[17] Pope was sufficiently pleased with the success of these efforts to underwrite *Wheelman* magazine in 1882 and to install, as its editor, the young Samuel S. McClure, who subsequently founded and managed the distinguished *McClure's* magazine.[18] These publications and a flurry of press notices prompted an 1882 *Leslie's* article to observe, "Books, magazine articles, bicycling papers, the daily and weekly press have made the history and the uses of this modern carriage familiar everywhere."[19]

These enterprising efforts favored Stevens when he completed his trip across the United States and arrived in Boston atop his Pope Columbia. Without it the continuation of his trip around the world would never have happened. Stevens's expensive bicycle and travel expenses consumed a large amount of his modest savings. Though he benefited enormously from the generosity and hospitality of people along the way, the long voyage ahead and the unpredictable conditions of the next leg necessitated a hefty infusion of cash—and careful reformulation of his murky plans.

Earlier, when he had arrived in Chicago, Stevens informed a curious reporter that his projected route from Chicago would carry him through Toledo, Cleveland, Buffalo, Albany, and down the Hudson River with an anticipated finish in New York City. Already he was contemplating a continuation of his trip around the world, and he explained that he would sail from New York for England after a couple of weeks of rest and meet there with the publisher of his book.[20] However, when he reached Albany, he struck out for Boston instead. Stevens never explained his reasons for this amended destination, but it surely involved new awareness of the centrality of Boston and Colonel Pope to bicycling. Before he reached Chicago, he had applied for membership in the LAW and sent *Wheelman* magazine a long letter recounting his trying ordeal near Fort Bridger.[21] His subsequent rerouting was influenced even more by encounters with LAW members in Cleveland and Buffalo, who alerted him to Pope's involvement with the organization and his corporate headquarters in Boston.

The *Boston Post*'s extensive coverage of Stevens's momentous arrival there verify his cognizance of the importance of his bicycle: "The machine used was a 50-inch Columbia 'standard,' of which its rider speaks in high terms of praise."[22] To a reporter for the *Boston Globe* Stevens again voiced plans for continuing around the world that fall. Although this account observed that a "note book was strapped to the lead of his machine," Stevens did not mention any book and said only, "I am making the journey partly for pleasure and partly for other reasons."[23] Actually, Stevens did not depart for England until the following spring, more than seven months later, and when he did, he carried with him a 140,000-word manuscript account of his trip across the United States, which no American publisher wanted.

When Stevens opted for Boston, he was obviously hoping that Pope would be sufficiently impressed by his accomplishment and his Columbia bicycle to contribute financing. But he realized his mistake quickly. After a large banquet that included Pope and prominent locals, the manufacturer offered him only a shiny, nickel-plated, top-of-the-line Columbia Express.[24] If Stevens was disappointed, he may not yet have realized the problem his expectations posed. All of Pope's promotion was cued to bicycling as sport for amateurs. The bylaws of the LAW emphatically mandated: "The League is intended for the benefit of amateur wheelmen, an amateur being defined as 'a person who has never competed in an open competition, or for a stake . . . or pursued bicycling or other athletic exercises as a means of livelihood.'"[25] Long before he ever arrived in Boston, Stevens was aware of the LAW's vehement opposition to racing, and he had always assumed his opponent to be the uncertainties of the road ahead. Now with his bicycle safely sequestered in temporary storage, he slammed into his greatest obstacle so far: if Pope agreed to fund the next leg of his trip as Stevens had hoped, he would no longer be an amateur and thereby violate this cornerstone principle of Pope's business plans.

The reality and gravity of this problem are verified by two incidents from Stevens's completion of his trip around the world. In sharp contrast to his earlier praise for his Columbia

4. Bay Area Chapter of the LAW (*Stevens sitting at far right*).
(Bancroft Library, University of California, Berkeley, 1960.010:202 Ser.2Neg)

bicycle to the *Boston Post*, Stevens did not identify the manufacturer of his machine and was quoted as saying, "The
bicycle used by me on my travels has a fifty-four-inch wheel,
and I ask that the Chronicle would publish the fact that I am
not engaged in advertising any particular make of bicycle,
simply using that which I have for my own convenience."[26]
The virulent threat of professionalism and Pope's justified
wariness were confirmed even more by a dispute that immediately flared up between Stevens and the LAW. Having
ridden around the world with a patch of the organization
prominently displayed on his coat, Stevens fired off a letter to renew his lapsed membership as soon as he returned.
However, the LAW rejected it on grounds that he was no longer an amateur. As support, it cited a Boston race in which
Stevens participated prior to his departure for Europe.[27] This

event was planned as a display of long-distance riding rather than as an actual race, and the gate receipts, which were preannounced as support for Stevens, proved insignificant.[28] Nonetheless the LAW judged his participation to be reprehensible professionalism and denied his membership application. *Outing* sprang to Stevens's defense with publication of both letters and an editorial maintaining that Stevens had done nothing wrong. Acknowledging "the necessity of drawing the line [on professionalism], and drawing it sharply," it maintained that Stevens had "done more to advance the cause of *purely amateur cycling* in the eyes of the world at large than any one else in existence."[29]

Pope's initial withholding of sponsorship forced Stevens back to the book he had first mentioned in Chicago. In his *10,000 Miles on a Bicycle* (1887), Karl Kron (Lyman Hotchkiss Bagg) provides the most reliable record of Stevens's activities during the seven-month hiatus between his Boston arrival and his London departure:

> Stevens set about making his first serious effort with the pen; and, in the course of six or seven weeks, produced a narrative of some 38,000 words, which, by my advice, he sold to *Outing*, in whose columns it finally appeared (April, May, June, and July, 1885). . . . Encouraged by advance payment for this, he worked steadily on, from October to March, preparing a more elaborate sketch (about 140,000 words) of his cross-continent adventures: and then began to look around for some book-publishers who might buy the manuscript. Just at this time, Col. Pope, a chief stockholder in the magazine, having been impressed by his *Outing* articles and the genuineness of his ambition to really push a bicycle round the world, invited him up

to Boston, and commissioned him as a regular correspondent to complete the journey. . . . The exact details of the
arrangement are unknown to me.[30]

Despite its illuminating information, this account either
omits or glosses over several important items. First, Stevens
did not need Bagg to introduce him to *Outing*. Its September 1884 issue carried the letter that Stevens had sent to the
magazine from Omaha back in June. The four-month delay
between the mailing and actual publication may have been
due to an intentional withholding of this letter until his trip
was completed or the fact that it arrived at the time when
Pope was purchasing *Outing* and consolidating it with his
Wheelman.[31] Whatever the case, Stevens had no need for a
Bagg introduction. Next, there is Stevens's "140,000-word
manuscript," which represents much more than Stevens ever
published about his American trip and has never been seen.[32]

Still, the biggest flaw in Bagg's account involves his inadequate accounting for Pope's change of heart. He simply
states that Pope was "impressed" by Stevens's "*Outing* articles." Actually the rationale underlying the colonel's turnabout was more complicated. The first of Stevens's four articles about his trip across the United States did not appear
until April 1885, the same month that he left for England.
Thus Stevens had published only a single letter in *Outing*
before Pope hired him as a correspondent, and this decision
could not have been influenced by any response from the
magazine's readership. A brief notice in the November 1884
issue of *Outing* also establishes that Pope accepted Stevens's
first four articles long before they were actually published:
"We take special pleasure in announcing that we have completed arrangements with Mr. Stevens for a narrative of his

5. Thomas Stevens beating a horseman.
(From Stevens, *Around the World on a Bicycle*, 1:319)

journey, for exclusive publication in *Outing*. It will comprise four papers, of ten pages each. . . . We have no hesitation in saying that this will be the most important and interesting series of articles, from the wheelman's stand-point, that has yet appeared in the magazine."[33]

This initial notice was followed by several announcements of postponement and a key revelation in the issue preceding the one that carried the first: "With the April issue this magazine will begin a new series. Fifty pages will be added to its size, the compound title *Outing and the Wheelman* will be changed to the simple and expressive *Outing*, a new cover will be adopted, and several typographical improvements will be made."[34]

This statement reveals that Pope's amended decision to provide Stevens financial backing was closely tied to his ambitious expansion of *Outing*. This consolidation and new format, coming on the heels of one during the previous year, created a need for more content and earned Stevens a contract for additional installments on the continuation of his trip. Pope intentionally withheld publication of the first article on crossing America until the consolidation of his two magazines had been completed and his new format was ready. Since this article did not appear until Stevens was on his way to England, he had ample lead time to acquire and write up new experiences. These reports, which Stevens posted back from convenient points along the way, provided exciting news about his progress. Newspapers noticed the mounting interest in Stevens and relied on these reports and intermittent dispatches to generate more.[35] Best of all, by hiring Stevens for writing rather than riding, Pope preserved his amateur status.

A year later, while Stevens was still en route, Pope sold *Outing* at a loss of sixty thousand dollars.[36] Staggering though this setback was, it neither surprised nor disturbed him because he understood that good promotion was costly and now realized that Stevens's trip superbly complemented his earlier promotion. Not only had Stevens validated the capability and durability of his Columbia bicycle, but he had also authenticated all that a determined amateur might accomplish. Pope always believed that the most promising market for his Columbia bicycles was unskilled enthusiasts and vigorously promoted cycling as a participatory sport that did not require special ability or skill. As one contemporary article explained: "There is still some notion abroad that this is a difficult art to learn. It may be acquired by any one in five half-hours. Boys step to the bicycle from their velocipedes without hesitation. The young man learns more quickly; but none of active life or free use of limbs are too old to take it up and make it convenient and enjoyable."[37] Despite the extraordinary prowess that his accomplishment necessitated, Stevens consistently downplayed his riding ability. Most early reports about him stressed that his experience prior to his departure consisted of casual rides around San Francisco's Golden Gate Park. The *Boston Post* even quoted Stevens's claim that he had "become famous before becoming a skillful rider."[38] Stevens, of course, understood that such admissions made good copy. Whether or not he consciously realized their usefulness to Pope's objectives, their value registered.

Equally important to Stevens's accomplishment as an effective role model for bicycling was his robust health.[39] Besides his astounding resistance to disease and injury, reporters consistently noted how fit he appeared. Significantly, health was a centerpiece of Pope's bicycle promotion. An 1881 Pope catalog that provided information about Columbia models, dimensions, and prices featured a testimonial by a Dr. J. T. Goddard, who proclaimed: "Riding the bicycle affords pleasurable excitement. . . . It takes men out into the pure air, into God's light and sunshine, and braces their lungs with the very breath of heaven. . . . It is an inducement to young men who work in close apartments to spend more time in the open air, and furnishes them with a means of healthful, invigorating, and, at the same time, pleasant exercise, such as nothing else can possibly afford."[40] An article on "Uses of the Bicycle" in the first issue of *Wheelman* made this same point. "Bicycle-riding brings about a physical development of high order," it announced, and then proceeded to explain: "Harmonious exercise and development of the body are of greatest importance to promote and sustain health; and for this use the bicycle is scarcely equalled among athletic exercises."[41] Central to this preoccupation with health was an emergent belief that men were overworked and in need of therapy. The best corrective was exercise *and* escape from the conditions responsible for this problem. The bicycle accomplished both by taking its rider into the outdoors and away from the debilitating effects of urban, industrial life. In fact, the first issue of the enlarged *Outing* cited this objective as its raison d'être:

> Because men are over-worked, and the nerves of women are strained to the highest possible tension, and even merry childhood is too often driven with whip and spur to the development of the brain, and shamefully neglected as to symmetry and vigor of body, there is room for us and work for us. . . . Intensity of labor demands regularity in recreation if the human frame is to bear the strain. To promote the higher recreation, and inspire men and women with an enthusiasm for out-of-doors, is the mission and the purpose of this magazine.[42]

This concern for fresh air and the outdoors accorded special value to getting away from cities to an unspoiled environment and elemental experience. The *Boston Globe*'s headline characterization of Stevens as "Cowboy and Cyclist" and the *Boston Post*'s description of him as "tanned to the color of a Sioux Indian" effectively verified these claims.[43] Stevens's trip not only carried him away from the dangers and debilities of civilized existence but also brought him into contact with nature and its therapeutic restoration of vibrant health. If his body benefited from the exercise and became more robust, the challenge and demand of this new environment made him a more resourceful, self-reliant person. In other words, many of the traits that made Stevens so remarkable came from opportunities afforded by his magnificent bicycle.

Stevens's trip affirmed additional benefits of bicycling. In his article "Uses of the Bicycle," C. E. Hawley argued that bicycling stimulated a cordiality that made riders more sociable. As he explained, "On the wheel the grave become gay, the reticent expand and become communicative, and the better and kindlier feelings of our nature are roused."[44] According to this logic, bicycling naturally fostered interest in the clubs that Pope had founded and was supporting. Hawley implied that this collegiality diminished concern for status and allayed class conflict. A friendly acceptance of others was a natural consequence of a bicyclist's revitalized spirits; his bicycle brought him into contact with an enlarged range of people and inspired cordial exchange. In comments that predated Stevens's trip but illuminate its significance for Pope, Hawley characterized the bicyclist as an ideal ambassador of good will: "Every peaceful traveller to foreign countries is a mite added to the closer communion of nations; and when he carries with him and receives the active sympathies of bicycling, his influence is greater than that of diplomacy."[45] However much Stevens's effectiveness with strangers came from his working-class background and traits peculiar to him, this promotion suggested that his bicycle was a key factor in his success.

At the center of all this promotion lurked several glaring ironies. The bicycle that whisked Stevens away from blighted urban, industrial culture was itself a product of that culture. However flawed that culture may have been, Pope still believed that it was superior to other cultures of the world and that the bicycle attested to this superiority. Each year during the 1880s his trade catalogs placed more and more emphasis on the industrial craftsmanship and finely tuned precision of his product. The 1880 accounting of his bicycle's many features culminates with an assertion that "its manufacture [was] one of the great industries of the world." The sophisticated engineering of its component parts refuted any claim that the bicycle was frivolous. It was a product of American know-how and a testimonial to its accomplishment. With unchecked chauvinism, the brochure boasted, "This is the product of American industry [of] which all who are truly American should be proud."[46]

This promotion also obscured the important fact that Stevens never considered himself a weakened product of industrial culture nor a distressed fugitive from it. On the contrary, it endowed him with an unshakable confidence in his strength and superiority. He resolutely believed that his culture had prepared him for the formidable challenges of his trip. As he explains at one point: "I bowl along southward, led by a strange infatuation of a pathfinder, traversing terra incognita, and rejoicing in the sense of boundless freedom and unrestraint that comes of speeding across open country where Nature still holds her primitive sway" (2:125). As his reference to himself as "a pathfinder" suggests, his appreciation for nature and primitive conditions bespeaks a sensibility conditioned by civilization and committed to it. This bias is even more apparent in his response to the diverse people he encountered. Stevens sincerely liked and accepted them; the fact that he was seldom stranded without food or shelter amply attests to his broad outreach and his sincere gratitude for the meager fare he was offered. Of course, his like or dislike of people was heavily influenced by their responses to him and his adamant belief in the superiority of Anglo-American culture. As one might expect, he was very critical of the hostile residents of Persia and China. Yet toward even those who accepted and/or aided him Stevens harbored a distinct sense of personal superiority that he usually (and wisely) reserved for his reader. He voices a frank, egalitarian aversion to privileged individuals who have no respect for merit and need: "How utterly unsatisfactory and altogether wretched seems even the gilded palace of a Persian provincial governor—the meaningless compliments, the salaaming lackeys and empty show of courtesy, when compared with the cosey quarters, the hearty welcome, the honest ring of an Englishman's voice, and the genuineness of everything" (2:94). While the impoverished and exploited are never judged so harshly, Stevens's partiality to his own culture does intrude on his efforts at understanding. "Hearts," he observes in a telling aside, "are none the less warm because hidden beneath the rags of honest poverty and semi-civilization." He then adds, "It takes but little to win the hearts of these rude, unsophisticated people" (1:166).

As offensive as this cultural superiority and condescension can be to a modern sensibility, it was undeniably crucial to the success of Stevens's trip. However much Stevens strove to be the classless ambassador of good will in Pope's publicity, he steadfastly believed that he and his bicycle were products of the world's most advanced culture and that this culture had prepared him for the challenges and adversities of his trip. Again and again locals warned Stevens of forbidding obstacles, lurking bandits, destinations fraught with danger. Convinced that these warnings said more about the speakers than the conditions ahead, Stevens refused to be deterred. As he explains at one point: "Warnings of danger have been repeated so often of late, and they have proved themselves groundless so invariably that I should feel the taunts of self-reproach were I to find myself hesitating to proceed on their account" (1:424–25). Of course, some warnings were legitimate, and when the predicted danger did materialize, Stevens simply trusted his acculturated resourcefulness. After fording a menacing stream that intimidated locals, he observes, "They now regard me as a very dare-devil and determined individual, a person entirely without fear" (2:169). As he explains earlier in a telling observation, "These people cannot possibly understand why it is that an Englishman or American, knowing of danger beforehand, will still venture ahead" (1:163), and he later proclaims, "I scarcely anticipate any [difficulties] that time and perseverance will not overcome" (1:222).

Stevens describes instances where his unshakable confidence could easily have worsened his problems and perhaps ended his life. On at least three occasions he recklessly lashed out at threatening individuals (1:363, 412; 2:188). When the

son of an unfriendly pasha disregarded his repeated requests
not to touch his bike, Stevens seized him and hurled him into
a ditch (1:441). More typically, however, this boldness and
daring were tempered by a circumspect caution. One telling
example of this is the evolution of his attitude toward another product of his industrial culture: his pistol. Despite the
acute restriction of his bicycle, Stevens elected to carry a gun
the whole trip. Presumably this was a defense against menace, but during the early stages, it was more an amusement
as he fired away at animals without regard to the threat they
posed. "There isn't a day that I don't shoot at something or
other," he reflects at one point, "and all I ask of any animal is
to come within two hundred yards and I will squander a car-
tridge on him" (1:40). But he quickly learned that it was better to keep his gun stowed. For the increased dangers beyond
Constantinople, he purchased a lighter, better-made Smith
and Wesson. After encounters with ominous figures flourishing ancient rifles and suspect swords, he concluded that he
too should display his weapon, especially since his gun was
"as superior to their armaments as [was] a modern gunboat
to the wooden walls of the last century" (1:275–76). But he
discovered that this tactic was more a provocation than a
deterrent, and he stowed his weapon and went for it only as a
last resort. In the rare instances in which he actually fired, he
did so to warn and frighten, never to kill (1:405, 452; 2:120).
"Had I killed or badly wounded one of them," he acknowledges with characteristic understatement, "it would probably
have caused no end of trouble or vexatious delay" (1:405).
Stevens responded to armed natives and potential thieves as
he did to other adversities: he adamantly refused to be deterred and then pushed ahead with vigilance and caution.

6. Cover, Columbia Bicycle catalog.
(Connecticut Historical Society, 629.22 P826h 1880)

Pope's vision of the ideal rider of his Columbia Standard presumed upon features of the "gentleman amateur" but involved a class issue that made him distinctively different. Although the colonel targeted both his bicycles and his clubs at a level above the working class, his support for Stevens clearly demonstrated that workers were acceptable—as long as they aspired to being more than merely that. As an enthusiast of classless recreation, Pope's democratic cyclist actively subverted the elite status that the "gentlemen amateur" had always taken for granted. This radical idea arose naturally from America's industrial expansion and Pope's involvement with business, and Stevens's trip reveals how quickly it was developing into a cornerstone tenet of sport as well.

The success of Stevens's ride and publications fulfilled his dream of escaping his drab life and gained him an opportunity to become a journalist. Drawing yet again upon his daring and resourcefulness, he proposed to ride a horse through a remote area of Russia, which he had previously considered and rejected as an alternative route around Afghanistan. His experiences were recounted in a book titled *Through Russia on a Mustang* (1891). Next, when Sir Henry Morgan Stanley, the man who "found" David Livingstone, was himself reported missing in central Africa, Stevens persuaded the *New York World* to hire him to undertake a search. His dispatches were the first reports to confirm that the explorer was alive and well. By this point he had arrived at the inevitable realization that extreme adventure was sport for younger men. Needing less risk and more security, he married the widowed mother of two famous English actresses, Violet and Irene Van Brugh, and lived out the rest of his career as business manager for the Garrick Theatre in London.

TWO

Fanny Bullock Workman

Mountaineering as Science and News

At a December 1907 meeting of the Royal Geographical Society (RGS) in London, Dr. William Hunter Workman presented a talk on a climb he had taken with his wife into the Nun Kun area of the Himalayas. Having previously toured numerous countries with her on bicycles and recently completed their fifth Himalayan expedition, he was honored to be addressing this venerable organization, which dated back to 1830 and included among its membership famous adventurers like Charles Darwin, Richard Francis Burton, and David Livingstone. As Americans the Workmans knew that RGS recognition for their achievements would be difficult to obtain, and they had been actively currying it for several years.

In his introduction to this address, Sir George D. Taubman Goldie, the current president, observed that to date only three climbers—Workman, his wife, and another RGS member in attendance—had reached elevations beyond 23,000 feet (7,000 meters). "I shall not enter into the difficult question as to what traveler has ascended the greatest height above sea level," he proclaimed. "But I will remind you that all these explorers are not merely trying how high they can climb. Careful observations are taken of glaciation and in other scientific directions, so that their ascents have real scientific value."[1] Extending his efforts to promote a genial atmosphere, Goldie humorously glossed the conspicuous absence of Fanny Workman by explaining that she was away in Germany doing "something more arduous than climbing 23,000 feet"—giving thirty lectures in thirty-seven days.[2] The RGS's policy of excluding women from membership and allowing them only as invited guests sent Fanny elsewhere to talk about her mountaineering successes. Six years later, the year she completed her seventh and final trip into the Himalayas, the RGS finally eliminated its barrier against women and included her in the first group of women to be awarded membership.

These expeditions affirmed Fanny's ambition and daring, but it was her numerous publications and their attentiveness to "glaciation" and "other scientific directions" that earned her the attention and respect of the RGS. Some members would fault her for flaunting of her limited scientific knowledge and her attacks on the inaccuracies of rivals, but she consciously and willfully did so in order to convince the organization of her close adherence to its standards for achievement. President Goldie, as head of this eminent gentleman's club, preferred to stand up for the cause of science and to avoid petty technicalities like which climber actually attained the highest elevation. Fanny, on the other hand, was fiercely competitive and intent on records, and she believed that the best way to achieve satisfactory recognition was to treat the RGS as the foremost authority, cue her efforts to its expectations, and win approval.

English enthusiasm for mountaineering was one reason that the RGS loomed so large in the sport. Even more important was the society's longstanding commitment to exploring and mapping the unknown. As originally judged by this standard, mountain climbing was vigorous recreation. Several centuries of evolving esthetics had transformed the prevailing view of mountains from that of diabolic wastes to sublime wonders, but most converts to this alternative view preferred admiring them to scaling them. However, the popularity of summer climbs in the Alps among Englishmen led to Edward Whymper's first summiting of the Matterhorn in 1865, an event that received widespread attention because three members of his party fell to their deaths on the trip down.

Over the years that followed, this costly triumph spurred climbers to try more-menacing peaks and new routes up ones that had already been conquered. As the untracked expanses of jungle, desert, and tundra diminished, high peaks in ever more remote locations suddenly loomed larger and more challenging. Two presidential reports in the RGS's *Geographical Journal* reveal how these developments altered its view of mountaineering. The first, from 1893, catalogs a broad array of countries with "geographical problems that remain to be solved." Although this report mentions the mountain ranges of New Zealand, the Andes, and the Himalayas and even remarks that "a glorious field is open to the mountaineer," its author clearly does not consider the conquest of peaks a valid reckoning with "geographical problems." However, an ensuing report from 1896 — only two years before the Workmans embarked on their first expedition into the Himalayas — focused on this region and offered an extensive account of the ranges that remained unexplored and unmapped.[3]

Wealth and status greatly aided Fanny's attraction to sport. She was born in Worcester, Massachusetts, into a prominent, well-to-do family, which assured her a life of comfort and security. Her father, Alexander Hamilton Bullock, came from Pilgrim heritage and was elected mayor of Worcester and then governor of Massachusetts. He married Elvira Hazard, whose father was a prosperous Connecticut landowner and cofounder of a successful gunpowder company. When Elvira's father died, her inheritance made Alexander one of the wealthiest men in Massachusetts.[4] Consequently, Fanny was schooled by private tutors and sent to Miss Graham's, an elite finishing school in New York City. From there she went to even fancier schools in Paris and Dresden, where she became fluent in French and German and developed a facility with foreign languages crucial to her future.

Early on, Fanny chafed at the constraints of her privilege. The scant evidence from this early period includes a handful of stories affirming an early enthusiasm for adventure and writing. One of these, titled "A Vacation Episode," is about a young, beautiful, aristocratic English girl who is bored with her peers and resistant to their suffocating expectations. With her ample funds, she bolts for the mountains near Grindelwald, Switzerland, and strikes out on a series of hikes into the mountains. This fiction was probably inspired by Fanny's own experience and perhaps a similar measure of rebellion. Even though Fanny's family may have sent her to Europe to match up with an aristocrat there, her headstrong English heroine upsets her parents by marrying an American. In 1881, when she was twenty-two and back from Europe less than a year, Fanny likewise agreed to marry a fellow American, but her choice of someone from her home town with equal status delighted her parents. William Hunter Workman was eleven years older, a graduate of Yale, and like his own father, trained as a doctor at Harvard Medical School. Their wedding was a major social event attended by prominent New Englanders and duly reported in the *New York Times*.[5] This glamorous match involved more than pedigree. Between completion of medical school and commencement of his practice in Worcester, Dr. Workman attended several universities in Germany and like Fanny, harbored fond memories of his time there.[6]

Two years later, a daughter was born, but she was unable to calm the mounting restlessness of her parents. Their welling discontent over the limitation of provincial Worcester and the diversified allure of Europe was intensified by the deaths of their respective fathers. Alexander Bullock died a year after their wedding, and Workman's father succumbed two years later. These passings brought the couple enormous inheritances and severed William's commitment to his profession. The year after the death of his overbearing father, the couple went on an extended tour of Scandinavia and Germany. Two years later Dr. Workman announced that a debilitating illness had compelled him to close his medical practice and that he was relocating to Europe. Whether or not this illness was real, other factors spurred this important decision, and his health returned surprisingly fast.

At the time of her departure for Europe, Fanny was pregnant with a second child, and Siegfried was born in Dresden in 1889. Since the Workmans were more interested in traveling than raising a family, Siegfried was not even a year old when they left him and his older sister, Rachel, with nurses

8. Fanny Workman with her bicycle in India, 1898.
(National Library of Scotland, by permission of the MacRobert Trust)

in Dresden and embarked on a series of trips on the recently invented safety bicycle, whose popularity surged with the introduction of the pneumatic tire in 1888. "Bicycle Riding in Germany," one of Fanny's earliest articles, deals mostly with the variation in bicycle regulations from city to city there, but her conclusion shifted to the recent upsurge in women riders and her own realization of "what an interesting, exciting, and health-giving exercise bicycling is."[7] This conclusion suggests that she and William may have taken up bicycling for their health, she to recover from the birth of her second child, and he to overcome the ailment that had ended his career.

What started as invigorating excursions to nearby cities quickly evolved into venturesome cycling through other

35

countries: Italy, France, and Switzerland. Following their return from Sicily in 1893, Siegfried contracted influenza, which deteriorated into pneumonia and took his life. One commentator has validly conjectured that the Workmans dealt with this unfortunate death by pursuing a "Flying Dutchman life."[8] Only four months after the funeral, the couple departed for Algeria and a bicycle trip that took them "over the Atlas to the Sahara," as Fanny's account was subtitled. The following spring they toured Spain. In 1896 they cycled Egypt, with shorter visits to countries en route there.[9] These excursions affirm that Fanny's enthusiasm for adventure and sport was truly exceptional for a woman of her era.

Fanny was also seeking more than healthy exercise, liberation from painful memories of her son, and an escape to the exotic. Prior to Siegfried's death, she quietly ignored prevailing expectations that married women devote themselves to raising a family. Afterward, she aggressively pursued an alternative identity, one that liberated her from the conventional responsibilities of wife and mother and allowed for *her* interests and ambitions. Like Thomas Stevens, she seized upon the bicycle's popularity as an opportunity for personal validation and recognition. Although the challenges in her trips to Algeria and Spain paled alongside those in Stevens's tour of the world, they likewise strengthened her belief in her cultural superiority and the literary promise of her material.

Fanny and William jointly authored their books about cycling as well as the ones about the Himalayas, but she always did most of the writing. Initially William represented their interests. From November 1894 through March 1895, he wrote a series of letters to the English publisher Thomas Fisher Unwin in which he pointed out how little had been written in English about Algeria and argued that the popularity of bicycling assured readership for their account.[10] Both he and Fanny knew that Unwin favored new authors, having already published early works by Conrad, Galsworthy, and Wells. Since his ascent of the Matterhorn as a young man, Unwin had also been publishing books on travel and adventure.[11] However, he only accepted their offering on condition that they agree to pay the cost of publication. In his letter of agreement, William explained that he did not expect to recoup his investment but very much wanted their *Algerian Memories* to be available for his "many friends" in the United States—effective proof that the couple's trips were not frivolous indulgences.[12]

The Workmans pressed Unwin for a completed contract before they left for Spain. Unfortunately, their *Sketches Awheel in Fin de Siècle Iberia* (1897) was an ill-considered step backward. The Spain they called Iberia was rustic, quaint, and charming—as it had long been in numerous other travel books. Fanny was wise enough not to repeat her estimate of Algeria and claim that Spain was little known or badly misunderstood, but her determined quest for romance came across as strained and more than a little pompous. Again she favored bucolic beauty over the blighted conditions of cities. Even though development here was more pervasive, greatly reducing the opportunities for discovery and daring, mistreatment of women was equally commonplace and she found plenty more examples to decry. Fanny elected not to write a book about her trip to Egypt because she probably realized that she could not depend on her bicycle to spark interest in that country's overworked tourist attractions.

At this point the Workmans opted for the truly exotic and its opportunity for untouched subject matter. In November 1897 they departed from Marseilles for a two-and-a-half year circuit of India and adjacent countries. Over the first half of 1898, they peddled four thousand miles from the southernmost tip of the country to the high peaks in the north. Wanting her book to be as original as possible, Fanny devoted special attention to India's abundant ancient architecture, which shaded the adventurous vagabonding in her previous accounts toward an exercise of a discerning taste. This amended sensibility moved her to hire an English majordomo to manage luggage and arrange comfortable accommodations, an addition that was supposed to reduce mishaps and inconveniences, but this plan backfired when the valet proved unreliable and a harbinger of worse problems.

The Workmans planned their elaborate itinerary in order to reach the cool mountains and go trekking as summer heat seared the rest of India. This outing took them over several passes between 14,000 and 18,000 feet and a treacherous rope bridge to Askole, nicknamed "world's end."[13] The greatest challenge of this adventure proved to be the coolies, who were unremittingly slow and uncooperative, though far better than the ones the Workmans hired for a reconnaissance of the area around the 28,165-foot Kangchenjunga, the world's third highest mountain (and not conquered until 1955).[14] They arranged for Rudolph Taugwalder, a relative of the two Taugwalders who accompanied Whymper on his ascent of the Matterhorn, to come from Zermatt to be their guide. Although the Workmans started with provisions for six weeks, their porters revolted when they reached snow three days out and forced a return to Darjeeling. "We were powerless against what appeared like systematic opposition," Fanny would later declare.[15]

Why the Workmans, at this juncture in their travels and at the ages of fifty and thirty-nine, forsook their bicycles for climbing is a question not easily answered. Fanny claimed that they were smitten by the breathtaking scenery beyond Srinagar and wanted a closer look. However, Taugwalder was surely booked well before their departure from Marseilles, and William had already applied for membership in the Royal Scottish Geographical Society, the first of their many memberships in elitist organizations associated with mountain climbing. Undoubtedly, they had also read the RGS's recent publication on the opportunities of the Himalayas. Moreover, the couple had already done considerable climbing together. During their years in Worcester, the Workmans took many summer trips into the White Mountains, and their bicycle books are peppered with knowledgeable references to Mount Blanc, Monte Rosa, and Macugnaga.

This longstanding enthusiasm for climbing was no more important than Fanny's perception of the acclaim that another American woman (more on her later) was garnering from popular lectures about her ascent of the Matterhorn, which Fanny herself accomplished back in 1896.[16] Since her trip to Algeria, Fanny had been using bicycling to advance her reputation, and she probably realized the waning prospects for this kind of material.[17]

Whatever motivated this abrupt conversion to mountaineering, the disastrous first expedition would surely have ended any superficial interest. Early on, both Workmans realized that coolies were essential to success and a formidable problem. In the Himalayas climbers could neither obtain

9. Matthias Zurbriggen and Fanny Workman, 1899.

supplies along the way nor carry adequate amounts for their needs. Coolies, on the other hand, disliked frigid weather and menacing terrain and could not grasp their appeal to foreigners. This kind of interest was alien to their culture and orders from women even more so. This entrenched resistance was as much of an obstacle as the mountains, and both necessitated a steeled determination. The severe, upper-class manner of the Workmans and their forthright condescension toward "inferior" cultures probably did offend porters, and Kenneth Mason, a respected authority on the Himalayas, once commented: "The Workmans were, on their journeys, the victims of their own faults. They were too impatient and rarely tried to understand the mentality of the porters and so did not get the best out of them. . . . Some of the trouble experienced by later travelers can be traced to this unsympathetic attitude of the Workmans."[18] However, early English climbers did not treat porters much better, and most had similar problems. If Fanny berated recalcitrant coolies, as she later did her mountaineering rivals, her exasperation at their low regard for women and consequential unresponsiveness to her would have driven her to do so, and it is hard to believe that she would have fared better had she been less confrontational and demanding.

Over the nine months between their first trek into the Himalayas and their 1899 return, none of the Workmans' preparations was more important than their recruitment of Matthias Zurbriggen, the finest, most experienced guide of the era. He was with Sir Martin Conway on his pioneering 1892 expedition into the Karakoram area of the Himalayas. In 1894 he accompanied Edward FitzGerald on his expedition to climb Mount Cook, New Zealand's highest peak. When locals learned of this objective and beat him there, FitzGerald settled for first ascents of Mount Sealy, Mount Tasman, and Mount Sefton and afterward allowed Zurbriggen to solo Cook. During an ensuing assault on Aconcagua in Chile, the highest mountain in the Southern Hemisphere,

FitzGerald was overcome with altitude sickness, but he gallantly urged Zurbriggen to continue, allowing him to be the first to reach its summit. Since FitzGerald had no need for Zurbriggen in 1899, Conway contacted him on behalf of the Workmans.[19] In his *From the Alps to the Andes* (1989), Zurbriggen describes how he normally subjected prospective clients to a careful evaluation, but he did not do so with the Workmans because they had strong endorsements, their objective was enticing, and they paid very well.[20] When Zurbriggen first met Fanny in Srinagar, he understood immediately that she was after not just high peaks but record elevations.

In Askole, the Workmans hired fifty coolies and struck out for the Biafo Glacier, which Zurbriggen had previously visited with Conway. Massive melting over the intervening eight years had produced fields of seracs and crevasses that made progress slow and arduous. Next, menacing weather forced the group to retreat and reassess. The Workmans relocated to the less explored Skoro La Glacier and the high, unclimbed peaks surrounding it. Exceptionally fine weather on the second day enabled them to reach an 18,600-foot summit with breathtaking views of the Karakoram Range and Masherbrum off in the distance. Fanny's naming this mountain Siegfried Horn was an obvious memorial to her dead son, but her published account explains that *Sieg* was for success and *Friede* meant peace.[21] Atop this peak on this special day, she rejoiced at having gone higher than any woman so far.

Assured that Fanny was strong and fearless, Zurbriggen selected a neighboring peak that was even higher and more challenging. From an overnight camp at 17,000 feet, the group zigzagged across icy snowfields and cautiously inched up a final 60-degree incline to the summit. After determining the mountain's elevation to be 19,450 feet and naming it Mount Bullock Workman, Fanny was eager to push higher still. The final climb of a grand dome named Koser Gunge necessitated a return for fresh coolies and establishment of a new base camp. A sudden break in a prolonged stretch of foul weather allowed the Workmans, Zurbriggen, and two of the strongest porters to start early and camp overnight almost a thousand feet higher than any of their bivouacs so far. After a morning struggle up a sheer 1,200-foot wall, the snow basin beyond looked easy, but developing clouds, powerful winds, and icy footing kept it from being so. During the precipitous final ascent, Fanny's fingers got so numb she could no longer grip her ice ax and one of the coolies undid his rope and started crawling down. Propelled to the summit by adrenalin and desperation, the foursome lingered only long enough for their instruments to assess that the temperature was ten degrees Fahrenheit and their elevation was 21,000 feet.[22]

On these mountains, Fanny was slow, relentless, and intrepid. Bearlike, she solidly planted one foot and then groped for another secure grip with the other. At the time she lacked the pitons, carabineers, and special equipment that enabled later climbers to attack far more challenging stretches. Fanny's best guides possessed limited technical skills, but they compensated with a wealth of experience and judgment that enabled them to discern routes that she could manage. Fanny's greatest assets were her dauntless persistence and her immunity to altitude sickness. Above seventeen thousand feet, climbers commonly experience intensifying dizziness and loss of strength; some develop edemas that can be fatal if they do not descend immediately. Because these effects can fell even the strongest and bypass those with far less stamina, they diminish the advantages that men routinely enjoy in other sports; high peaks level gender inequality. Although conditioning can prepare a climber for the exertion of pushing upward, it is no help against the effects of altitude. But, Fanny discovered, prolonged stays at levels of reduced oxygen could enable her body to adjust. On one of her trips, she remained more than a month above fifteen thousand feet with no consequential debilitation. Because her naturally slow pace made swift ascents impossible, her hopes for reaching ever higher altitudes necessitated one or more Spartan overnight camps that accommodated her slow progress, acclimated her to higher elevations, and replenished her energy. Ironically, Fanny's limitations revealed to her this cornerstone principle of high-peak mountaineering—even though she later found that the efficacy of this tactic diminished beyond twenty thousand feet.

Upon completion of these three climbs, which successively raised her record for elevation, Fanny immersed herself in promotion of her achievement. First, she posted in the *Scottish Geographical Magazine* an account that appeared in its October 1899 issue.[23] The next issued offered a much shorter report on Fanny's conquest of Koser Gunge.[24] In neither of these articles did she claim new records, but Zurbriggen did so for her in a hastily added appendix to his memoir, which came out a few months later. "I was delighted to have escorted a lady to this height [21,000]," he proclaimed, "for Mrs. Workman has climbed 4,000 feet higher than any other member of her sex, and I am the first guide who has been

10. William and Fanny Workman atop Mount
Bullock Workman, 1899.
(National Library of Scotland, by permission of the MacRobert Trust)

lucky enough to accompany a lady to such an altitude."[25]
A year later a review of the Workmans' *In the Ice World of
the Himalayas* (1900) in the *Scottish Geographical Magazine* duly noted, "In the course of the last tour, Mrs. Bullock
Workman established three consecutive world mountaineering records for women, viz., 18,600, 19,450, and 21,000
feet."[26]

Dr. Workman referenced these two expeditions in his application to the Royal Geographic Society and was granted
fellowship. Fanny invoked this association and her own acceptance into the Royal Scottish Geographical Society to
lend authority to their *Into the Ice World of the Himalayas*, following their names on the title page with initials that

signaled these affiliations.[27] Over the pages that followed, Fanny strained to exhibit scientific knowledge with lengthy discussion of her innovative instruments and their operation. Proclaiming that her state-of-the-art Hicks Watkin Patent barometer had "remarkable precision," she maintained that the elevations offered by other climbers were usually flawed because they relied on older, less accurate aneroids and hypsometers. She added that most errors ran to the high side, and even Zurbriggen's three-inch Cary barometer was repeatedly one hundred to two hundred feet high at elevations over seventeen thousand feet.[28] Unfortunately, knowledgeable reviewers were unimpressed by these suspect attempts at scientific expertise. "It is the personal experience rather than the scientific fact which is generally brought forward," remarked one reviewer.[29] Another for the RGS's *Geographical Journal* quipped more acerbically, "The book makes no pretensions to scientific value."[30]

Trips over the summers of 1902 and 1903 repeated the earlier pattern of disappointment followed by success. For the 1902 outing the Workmans chose the hitherto unexplored territory of the upper Chogo Lungma Glacier and left for it with eighty coolies and four tons of supplies. But three weeks of constant snow, which included a storm lasting sixty hours, limited climbing to day trips that never surpassed nineteen thousand feet. The 1903 expedition targeted the Hoh Lumba Glacier. Incorrectly charted by the Indian Trigonometrical Survey, it was barricaded by high, precipitous passes and virtually unexplored. Cyprien Savoye, who had accompanied the Duke of Abruzzi on his 1902 polar expedition, replaced Zurbriggen as guide, and he brought along Joseph Petigax, a colleague from Courmayeur. With another

army of porters and bountiful provisions, this entourage arrived at its base camp praying that the weather would be
better than the year before.

When barometers signaled favorable weather ahead,
Fanny, William, two guides, and two porters immediately
launched a well-planned assault. They camped the first night
at 16,200 and the second at 18,600 feet. They intended to
pass the third night above 20,000 feet, but an ailing porter forced them to settle for an accommodating plateau at
19,355 feet. At 3:00 a.m. the next morning, the sick porter
was left behind and the others commenced the final leg. Beyond a cornice at 21,770 feet, they encountered new snow
only a foot deep and quickly ascended a peak that measured
22,567 feet and added 1,568 feet to Fanny's record. At this
point William left his wife with the other porter and struck
out with his two guides for Pyramid Peak, a needlelike spire
that was the trip's main objective. Inching their way up its
steep, craggy sides, they arrived at a ledge outcropping by
noon.[31] After calculating his elevation to be 23,394 feet, Dr.
Workman abandoned the summit because, as he later explained, "The peak would have been our mausoleum, for we
could not have regained camp that night, and a night in the
open at that altitude would have meant certain death from
cold."[32] He also realized that his stopping point was 500
feet higher than the existing elevation record and that the
remaining distance was a monumental challenge, not bested
until 1949. The regrouped party reached camp after dark,
awoke early to clouds, and started immediately for the base
camp, which they reached as a blizzard broke and affirmed
the wisdom of their decisions to hurry down.

The Workmans immediately dispatched news of these

conquests to the Royal Geographical Society and finally garnered the recognition they had been seeking. In November
1904 William was invited to address the membership about
the experiences that he would develop into the first of his
articles to be accepted by the RGS's *Geographical Journal*.[33]
The following year the RGS invited Fanny, and her talk was
an even bigger coup. The *London Times* commented on the
unusualness of a woman addressing the RGS and reported a
frank admission from the society's president that he could
recall only a single other such instance. Defensively, he explained that few women had ever met the society's rigorous
requirements for scientific research, exploration, power of
physical endurance, and strong love of adventure.[34]

The *Geographical Journal*'s ensuing publication of Fanny's "First Exploration of the Hoh Lumba and Sosbon Glaciers: Two Pioneering Ascents in the Himalayas" validated
her boastful title and flaunted her much improved scientific
expertise. At the outset she reported:

> This region, the glaciers of which were explored by us,
> lies between 74° 55' to 75° 45' E. long. and 35° 45' to 36°
> N. lat. . . . . From Skardu, the chief village of Baltistan, a
> march north-east brings one to the Shigar valley, which
> is traversed in 20 miles to its junction with the Braldoh
> and Basha rivers. . . . As you look down from the glacier,
> the river is seen to have cut its way between the hill and
> the moraine on the left. No signs of glaciation on the hill
> beside the stream were noticed, but the rock is weathered,
> and easily split, and striation marks would have been long
> since effaced. Another sign of retreat is the presence of an
> important moraine ridge, the highest point of which is 50
> feet above the glacier.[35]

This concentration of technical information and terminology was developed specifically for the readership of this journal and a striking departure from the romantic descriptions in her bicycling books. Unfortunately, this ostentatious display of authority greatly diminished the popular appeal of her books on the Himalayas that followed.

These successes did not diminish the Workmans' drive to push even higher. After a two-year hiatus the couple returned to Srinagar in the spring of 1906 for an expedition into the Nun Kun area, a hundred miles east. With Savoye again as guide, six porters from the Italian Alps, two hundred coolies, and massive supplies, the caravan situated a base camp in the midsection of the Nun Kun, where exceptionally fine weather allowed the climbers to reconnaissance a nest of jagged peaks rising up to twenty-five thousand feet.

The planned assault involved a sequence of four camps extending from a first one at 17,657 feet to a final one slightly above 21,000. For the last leg the climbers split into two groups. After concluding that the highest peak was inaccessible, William and a porter went after the second highest, but ominous clouds compelled them to retreat.[36] With Savoye and another porter, Fanny, currently forty-five years old, pursued an alternative spire that she named Pinnacle Peak and successfully reached its summit. She computed its altitude to be 23,263 feet, 130 feet lower than William's record on Pyramid Peak and thus no threat to their marriage.[37]

Having both cracked the 23,000-foot/7,000-meter barrier, the Workmans moved to establish themselves as *the* foremost authorities on thin air. Their articles maintained that climbers could not acclimate to conditions above 21,000 feet and would instead develop debilitating ailments. The first

11. Fanny Bullock Workman on Silver Throne.

and foremost problem was lack of oxygen, which made exertion harder and more taxing. Even worse than the numbing cold was the astounding range of temperature over the course of a single clear day; during the summer at 21,000, it regularly fell to below zero overnight and soared beyond one hundred degrees Fahrenheit by midafternoon.[38] Sleep deprivation, they argued, was an even greater hardship. No one in their group had been able to sleep during the final night of the Hoh Lumba ascent because the need for oxygen kept them in an upright position; anyone attempting to recline felt as though he were suffocating. During the three nights they spent above 19,900 in the Nun Kun, only one of the nine European members contracted the mountain sickness that incapacitated many porters, but all did not sleep and developed "mountain lassitude." "When the highest peaks of 28,000 and 29,000 are seriously attacked," Fanny projected, "more will fail through sleeplessness and its effects than any other cause."[39]

The following year, in June 1907, Thomas G. Longstaff reached the 23,406-foot summit of Trisul in the Garhwal-Kumaon area of the Himalayas, an accomplishment that surpassed William's record by twelve feet. Like Workman, Longstaff had abandoned a medical practice to climb mountains. He was both solidly ensconced in the elite English society to which the Workmans aspired and more drawn to risk. In 1905 he secured, through a diplomatic liaison, permission to enter forbidden Tibet for an extended trek that included a climb of Gurla Mandhata. When a poorly calculated push left his group short of the summit late in the day, he elected to bivouac on a nearby ridge, but the crossing to it set off an avalanche that swept him and his companions down 3,000 feet. Unbelievably, no one was harmed, and the group spent two nights in snow holes before giving up on their objective.[40] For Trisul, Longstaff used a base camp at 16,750 feet. When several days of nasty weather finally broke, his party left camp well before dawn, raced to the summit, and was back by 7:00 p.m.—a round trip of almost 7,000 feet each way. This audacious assault left Longstaff no time for altitude measurements at the top. "Rush tactics had certainly been vindicated this time," he later explained.[41]

Six months later, at an RGS event that President Goldie opened with an appeal for cordiality, Longstaff ventured a polite disagreement with Dr. Workman that swiftly turned contentious. When Goldie stated his reluctance to judge which climber had reached the highest elevation, he was well aware that two of the leading candidates were present. His well-intentioned attempt to thwart possible tension between them over this matter failed and served notice that mountain climbing was ceasing to be a gentlemanly endeavor and turning into serious, fractious competition. If Goldie's initial flourish of cordiality successfully diverted Longstaff and Workman from their own accomplishments, he was unable to prevent the eruption of an acrimonious dispute between them over the elevations attained by two other climbers—W. W. Graham and William Henry Johnson—forty years before. In an article prior to his address, Workman referenced a lingering belief that Graham had reached twenty-four thousand feet and proclaimed it to be unsubstantiated, but he had not commented on Johnson either in his articles or in his talk.[42] Longstaff began his postaddress comments with high praise for Fanny and "the extraordinary degrees of fortitude and perseverance with which she [was] gifted."[43] Disregarding his own recent achievement, he observed that the honor for the highest camp should go to Johnson, who "spent a night at over 22,000 feet," a claim that Workman rebutted as unproven. Longstaff next voiced skepticism about Workman's comments on the problems of thin air and conjectured that the summit of Everest might be reached with a single overnight at 19,000 feet and "rush" tactics like the ones both he and Johnson had employed.[44]

Several months before this confrontation, *Appalachia* magazine ran a letter from Fanny titled "Highest Camps and Climbs," which demonstrated her belief that the gentlemanly standards of the RGS warranted closer oversight. In it she disputed an earlier Longstaff claim that he had achieved the highest overnight camp during his Trisul trip. Following indignant assertions that Longstaff's aneroid was smashed at the time and that he "greatly overestimated the altitude of his high bivouac," she huffed: "In these days, when a mountaineer is expected to ascertain heights attained by means of instruments used with due regard to recognized scientific methods, how much value has Mr. Longstaff's or any one else's personal opinion in the absence of all attempts at proper measurement, in fixing the altitude of a high point that may have been reached?"[45]

Whether or not this publication was a factor, Longstaff dispatched a letter right after Workman's address to the *Geographical Journal* in which he expressed outrage at William's claim that Johnson had "wrongly estimated" his elevation.[46] William countered with a testy retort that opened, "I would call Dr. Longstaff's attention to the desirability, when criticizing the statements of others, of defining his own position with more precision than he has done in this case." After pointing out the scant proof Longstaff supplied for his claims, Workman challenged him to present more-convincing evidence.[47]

To members of the RGS, a feud like this was embarrassing.

12. The Workmans on a bridge over the Indus River, 1908.

They understood how vanity often sparked impolite conduct and believed that collegial tolerance and acceptance were more important than who deserved the record. Longstaff and Workman were, of course, former doctors and bristly about their educations and expertise, but the underlying root of this dispute was more cultural. Longstaff was a privileged clubman who considered mountain climbing exhilarating sport and was as cavalier about his risky tactics as he was about his lax measurements of elevation. The Workmans, on the other hand, were Americans, outsiders, and as competitive as they were wealthy. As much as they valued their ties with the RGS and did not want to appear mean spirited, they wanted this prestigious club to monitor more closely its standards of achievement.

The greatest consequence of these barbed exchanges by

far was its foreshadowing of a worse and more public spat between Fanny and Annie S. Peck. Peck was a fellow American whose passion for mountaineering and records was as intense as Fanny's. Though Peck's New England heritage was equally distinguished, her immediate family could not afford to support her exceptional ambition. She taught in public schools for almost a decade before enrolling in the University of Michigan to major in Greek, and after several more years of teaching, she returned for an MA. In 1885 she was awarded a grant to attend the American School of Classical Studies in Athens, the first woman to win this honor. Afterward she taught Latin at Smith College for two years. By 1893 she had given up teaching, become an itinerant lecturer, and was successful enough to be included in *A Woman of the Century: Leading American Women in All Walks of Life* (1893), in which she characterized herself as a "profound classical scholar, distinguished archaeologist, and an accomplished musician."[48] This entry only mentions her interest in mountain climbing. During her stay in Greece, she climbed Parnassus, Hymettus, and Penticus, and from Smith she made several trips into the White Mountains. During an ensuing visit to California, Peck tried more demanding climbs, first Cloud's Rest in Yosemite and then Mount Shasta, where she camped in snow for the first time.[49]

During an 1895 return to Europe, Peck, who was already forty-five, climbed numerous Alpine peaks, including the Grossglockner, the Jungfrau, the Fünf-Finger-Spitze, and the Matterhorn.[50] These challenges not only increased her confidence and ambition as a climber but also brought her professional opportunity. During her addresses on the lecture circuit, she experimented with one on her conquest of the famous Matterhorn and discovered that this topic out-drew her learned addresses.[51] Sensing the promise of this new direction, she decided to shift away from well-known, much-climbed mountains to ones that were more challenging and more exotic. This thinking inspired an 1897 trip to Mexico to climb Orizaba, the highest peak in Mexico, and Popocatépetl, an active volcano.

As part of her preparation, Peck contacted an editor at the *New York Sunday World* and convinced him to under-write her expenses in return for an account of her climb, which, she realized, would also be valuable promotion for her lectures. Peck's successful conquest of Orizaba yielded a press notice proclaiming that she had reached the highest elevation ever achieved by a woman.[52] However, her ascent of "El Popo" confronted her with an unanticipated problem fraught with significance for her future: her trip was event-ful but not eventful enough. At a hotel at the base of the mountain, she invited several guests to accompany her, and to her surprise they accepted and brought along a basket of food for a picnic along the way. On the summit she encoun-tered a young boy from lunch, who had beaten the group by taking a shorter route. Peck's candid account was sprightly but unacceptable to the editorial staff of the *World*. Having already run announcements of Peck's adventurous conquest, they purged information that diminished her achievement and ran it with the headline "Miss Peck on 'Pop's Sum-mit — Thrilling Details on the Woman Mountain-Climber's Ascent."[53] Unlike the membership of the RGS, which favored exploration and science, Annie's audience expected exciting news and triumph. The newspaper that carried this story, as well as the ones that ran her ensuing reports, wanted

climbing to be daring sport, not leisurely recreation or ana-
lytic investigation. Editors and readers demanded that the
outcome be as momentous as that of other sporting contests.

Anxious that her next undertaking be more challenging,
Peck selected Bolivia's Mount Sorata (Illampu). Even though
this trip cost Peck a pittance compared to each one of Fanny's expeditions into the Himalayas, the price of her two
Swiss guides, science professor, equipment, and porters so
far exceeded her constrained resources that it took her four
years to raise adequate funding. Again newspapers aided her
with commissioned articles and helpful publicity. Notices
on her departure informed readers that her objective was
unclimbed and possibly the highest peak in South America.
"Mount Sorata will be a crowning experience to Miss Peck's
adventures," reported one account, "for her ambition is to
ascend the highest peak in this hemisphere, as well as to set
a pace for man."[54]

Unfortunately, this trip was as disastrous for her as the
Workmans' 1898 expedition to Kangchenjunga. Her porters
likewise revolted when the entourage reached snow, and the
others lost confidence. She adamantly wanted to continue,
but the professor and her guides would not. "What could
I do? Three men against me," she later explained. "I could
climb, but could not carry up tents, sleeping bags, etc. To
manage three men seemed beyond my powers."[55] In ensuing
reports betrayals by men would become a familiar refrain.

For her 1904 return Peck secured sponsorship from the
prestigious *New York Times*, but it was so inadequate that
she was forced to severely economize, hiring this time a local
guide and only a handful of porters.[56] On the very first day
this group got higher than the previous assault ever did, but

this good fortune evaporated when they went for the summit. During an especially treacherous section, the men wore out and argued against continuation. Resolved not to fail a second time, Peck seized the lead and headed straight up an imposing incline until she nearly stepped into some crusty snow thinly covering a crevasse. Turning around to confer, she discovered that her companions had unroped themselves and remained below. Crestfallen and well short of her objective, she again had to turn back and this time sought to salvage her honor with a dramatic account that the *New York Times* ran with a headline proclaiming, "American Woman Mountain Climber Tells How She Broke All Records."[57]

Peck resourcefully marketed her failure so that it enhanced her reputation. A notice, which she probably orchestrated, in the December 1904 issue of *Outing* burnished her setback and linked Annie with Fanny for first time: "Annie Peck and Mrs. Fanny Bullock Workman have been making new climbing records for women; the former recently scaled Mount Sorata in Bolivia, which is but a hundred feet or so lower than Aconcagua (highest of South American peaks) in Chile, mapped at 22,884 feet, and Mrs. Workman reached 22,585 in the Himalayas."[58] Without actually stating it, this announcement implied that Peck's "scal[ing]"of Sorata surpassed Fanny's conquest of the Chogo Lungma Glacier by 200 feet. At the time Peck was well aware that Mount Sorata was more than "a hundred feet or so lower" than Aconcagua. Dr. Tight, a science professor on her first trip, had calculated its height to be 21,300 feet, roughly 1,500 feet lower than Aconcagua.[59] This journalistic aggrandizement emerges from elsewhere in her accounts, such as her suspect claim that she climbed hundreds of feet without ever

MISS ANNIE S. PECK, A.M.

THE WORLD-FAMOUS MOUNTAIN CLIMBER, LECTURER, AND WRITER,
OFFICIAL DELEGATE OF THE UNITED STATES TO THE
INTERNATIONAL CONGRESS OF ALPINISTS, 1900,
PRESENTS THE FOLLOWING LECTURES

Each Illustrated by 100 or more Wonderful Views which cannot be Duplicated
in this Country. The Lectures may also be given without Illustrations

Bolivia and Mt. Sorata

Peru and Mt. Huascaran
See Harper's Dec. 1906
Panama and the Canal

Mexico, with Ascents of
Popocatepetl and Orizaba

The Passion Plays of
Europe

Also
Business Opportunities
in South America and the Pan-American Railway.

To the Summit of the
Matterhorn

Afoot and Alone in Tyrol

Switzerland, with Ascent
of the Jungfrau

Athens, The Acropolis,
and Ten other Lectures
on Greece

MISS PECK IN CLIMBING COSTUME

Holding a second degree from the University of Michigan, the first woman to study at the American School of Archeology in Athens, having occupied the Chair of Latin at Purdue University and Smith College, Miss Peck is called by competent judges one of the most scholarly and accomplished women in the United States. Practically single-handed and alone she has accomplished extraordinary tasks. She has ascended higher on this hemisphere than any other American man or woman—to a height of approximately 20,500 feet on Mt. Sorata, in Bolivia—while in Peru she has made one first ascent and explored a section of country practically unknown here.

Miss Peck may be addressed at Hotel Albert, New York

13. Handbill for Annie Peck's lectures, 1907.
(National Archives)

noticing that her companions had unroped and remained behind. In her future articles and discussions with reporters, Annie avoided further mention of Fanny and her climbs, but she continued to inflate her own achievements and to assume that no one would bother to cross-check them.

Had she been committed to Sorata, Peck would have gone

59

after its summit a third time. What she wanted more was a mountain even higher. Instead of wasting additional time and money on Sorata, she bolted from Bolivia for Yungay, Peru, in order to explore Mount Huascarán, which a local engineer had calculated to be twenty-five thousand feet. "Should his measurement prove correct," she wired the *New York Times*, "this is undoubtedly the highest mountain in this hemisphere, and its ascent would break the world's record for climbing."[60] More unreliable men betrayed and defeated four attempts upon Huascarán's twin summits, but realizing how much the prospect of a world record stoked interest in her plucky persistence, Peck willfully disregarded accuracy, exploited suspect estimates, and kept promoting Huascarán as higher than Aconcagua.[61]

Success undid this reckless tactic. Believing that her reliance on locals had doomed her four previous attempts, Peck concluded that she needed accomplished, veteran guides and recruited Gabriel and Rudolph Taugwalder, who had been with the Workmans on their disastrous first expedition into the Himalayas. In order to keep her group small and affordable, she hired only two of the best porters from her previous outings. On August 7, 1908, Peck launched her fifth attempt on Mount Huascarán, but late in the afternoon of the final ascent, she found herself still two hours and a thousand feet shy of the summit. Estimating that the risks were too great to continue, she opted to try again the next day, but the next morning members of her team and their supplies were too depleted to do so. Peck stumbled back to the village of Yoga and dispatched news that she had "ascended higher than any man or woman in the world."[62]

After a week of recuperation, the group set out again and

by amending its route reached the third camp of the previous expedition on the first day. Unfortunately, the wind blew so hard at the outset of the final leg that Peck herself questioned whether they should continue, but this time her guides urged her to do so. The precipitous incline and ferocious cold drained energy and frayed nerves. Annie asked Rudolph for her special pair of vicuña gloves, but he lost one to the wind during the exchange. Close to the summit, Peck stopped for an altitude reading, but the wind snuffed her hypsometer. Meanwhile, Rudolph flagrantly disregarded her specific orders and pressed ahead for the summit. By the time she arrived with Gabriel, the weather was so forbidding that she was only able to snap a photo. En route down, Rudolph lost two of his own gloves and developed frostbite, and Annie miraculously withstood several nerve-racking slips. Finally Rudolph tumbled, upended her, and would have swept both of them over a precipice had Gabriel not arrested their slide with his rope. As both Peck and Rudolph despaired for their lives, Gabriel remained a pillar of strength and became the first man to deliver at Annie's worst time of need.[63] When they finally reached Yungay, Rudolph went directly to the hospital, where his foot and several fingers were amputated. Meanwhile, Annie wired news of her success, and the front page of the *New York Times* informed its readership that she had finally reached the "26,000 foot" summit of Mount Huascarán.[64]

On her ascent of Mount Huascarán, Peck wore three suits of lightweight woolen underwear, two pairs of tights, two flannel waists, a cardigan jacket, two sweaters, canvas knickerbockers, and four pairs of woolen stockings.[65] All this clothing was weighty, constricting, and still far too

14. Annie Peck in climbing attire, 1908.

(From Peck, *Search for the Apex of America*, 347)

porous. A poncho she almost left behind proved invaluable against the frigid wind near the summit. In an early article titled "Practical Mountain Climbing," she advised women to wear appropriate clothing and disregard fashionable appearance. She urged that they avoid dresses and adopt the knickerbockers commonly worn by men. "For a woman in difficult mountaineering to waste her strength and endanger her life with a skirt is foolish in the extreme," she insisted both here and in her account of Huascarán.[66] Peck's outspoken campaign against dresses went beyond their impracticality. Her attire likened her so much to a man that she embellished her high-altitude mask with a mustache when she posed for a studio photograph. Having stayed up with men and then bested so many in the mountains, she did not mind being mistaken for one. Fanny Workman, on the other hand, always insisted on wearing a dress however much more difficult and dangerous it made climbing. She was as insistent and as peculiar in her views about appropriate attire as Annie, but her underlying rationale, ironically, was quite similar. Fanny seldom appears in the myriad photographs of her climbs, but in those where she does, she is always viewed from a distance where her dress stands out and distinguishes her from her male companions. She wanted viewers to know that a woman had integrated this conventional gathering of male climbers and that she too had reached the summit.

On the voyage back, Peck tempered her initial exuberance as she completed an article to fulfill a contract with *Harper's*. Over her lengthy accounting of her six assaults, Peck is more than a little surprising in not bothering to mention Huascarán's height. Then in the last paragraph of her article, she modestly states: "If, as seems probable, the height is 24,000 feet, I have the honor of breaking the world record for men as well as women."[67]

Had Peck rested her case with this article, her claim might never have been questioned. But she had learned enough about mountain climbing to know that the most respected authorities on mountaineering accomplishment were scientific and geographic journals, not newspapers or popular magazines. Thus she reworked her *Harpers*'s article and submitted it to the *Bulletin of the American Geographical Society*, which ran it in the June 1909 issue. Disregarding whether this American version of the *Geographical Journal* conferred with its English sister on matters like this, she, like Fanny in her first book on the Himalayas, flourished her scientific qualifications with extended discussion of the instruments she took and used.[68] Most of this account of her six Huascarán trips recycles her *Harper*'s narration until she arrives at her failed effort to light her hydrometer during the ferocious weather of her summiting and here she adds, "To break, perhaps the world's records and not be able to prove it was a great disappointment, but to return alive seemed still more desirable."[69] This expression of dismay is followed by additional commentary on methods of measurement and their reliability, which prepare for this amended conclusion: "If future triangulations, or observations, made on the summit of the south peak, which is probably a trifle higher, should prove, as I have hoped, the altitude of Huascaran to be 24,000 feet, I shall have had the honour of breaking the world's record for men as well as women."[70]

Prior to this publication, Fanny had been too far away, too preoccupied, or simply too aloof to notice Annie's flood of press releases about her records, but when she learned that Annie's article and unsubstantiated claim had been published by such a reputable journal, she was outraged. Since no one else was willing to check the authenticity of this claim, she decided that she herself would do so. Immediately she contacted a trio of distinguished French topographers, headed by M. de Larminat, who had produced the most reliable measurement of Aconcagua, and commissioned them to do the same for Huascarán. She probably influenced this announcement, which appeared in the June issue of the *Geographical Journal*: "Miss Peck, whose account of her ascent appears in the June number of the *Bulletin of the American Geographical Society*, considers that its height is about 24,000, and that it is thus the highest summit in the Andes; but as no point higher than 19,600 feet was determined instrumentally, the extent of the further climb being merely estimated, this claim must at present be received with reserve."[71] Whether or not she engineered this expression of skepticism, she actively campaigned to disseminate it. Two months later she returned to the United States for the first time in five years and went out of her way to engage reporters about Peck, to explain that Huascarán had only been measured to 19,600 feet, and to point out that "the remainder of the distance to the summit was estimated [by Peck]."[72]

Early in 1910 Fanny's topographers reported back that the north peak, the one Peck climbed, measured 21,812 feet, and the south peak was 22,187, roughly a thousand feet lower than Aconcagua and Pinnacle Peak. She immediately dispatched this information to the *Geographical Journal*, the *Bulletin*, *Scientific American*, and various newspapers.[73]

Next, she lodged a complaint about Peck's claims with the British Academy of Sciences, which ruled in her favor the following spring. "Mrs. Workman Wins" headlined an account of this decision.[74] Fanny established beyond doubt that she deserved the record for the highest elevation achieved by a woman, and she retained it for nine years beyond her death in 1925 — although a later, more precise instrumentation determined that Pinnacle Peak was actually 22,736 feet.[75] Even though Fanny discredited her claim, Annie returned a blow that was almost as damaging when she revealed that the cost for Workman's measurement was four times that of her entire expedition.[76]

Both women went on to climb more mountains, though none as high or as challenging as Pinnacle Peak and Huascarán. Fanny's book on her seventh and eighth expeditions into the Himalayas, *Two Summers in the Ice Wilds of Eastern Karakoram* (1917), has been judged by many then and since to be her best, though the reviewer for the *Geographical Journal* faulted its "constant disparagement of Dr. Longstaff."[77] Fanny's final expedition in 1912 kept her away from her daughter's wedding to a Scottish lord. She died at the age of sixty-six in Cannes, twelve years before William, who lived to be ninety. Peck continued to return to South America and sought to establish herself as an authority on its culture and commerce, first with *Industrial and Commercial South America* (1922) and later with *Flying over South America*. She remained professionally active up until her death in 1935 at the age of eighty-five and completed a climb in the White Mountains three years before.

The significance of the rivalry between Workman and Peck extends beyond their strident claims to have climbed higher than any other woman. Their ambitious pursuit of towering, unclimbed peaks in the remotest areas of the world (still so today) were conceived and executed as proof that women could be first-rate mountaineers and the equal of men at levels of thin air. Previously, mountain climbing had been a male preserve dominated by wealthy Englishmen, who viewed it as affirmation of their Saxon manhood and a meaningful extension of the empire. Fanny Workman and her husband were among the first to comprehend that the Himalayas constituted *the* greatest challenge and to deploy their substantial wealth to achieve record elevations there. Their accompanying quest for recognition of their accomplishment from the Royal Geographical Society and contentious publications contributed significantly to the sport's evolution from strenuous recreation into serious, regulated competition. Even though climbers today seldom bother to determine the elevation of their peaks, a remarkably large number of them continue to have an exceptional veneration of technology, one that is as quirky as it is scientific in its very strong opinions about gear and information gathering.

Peck, on the other hand, sorely lacked the Workmans' privilege and constantly had to battle her way around financial roadblocks. Her ambitious pursuit of advanced degrees and travel should have carried her away from the exorbitant expense of top-flight mountaineering, but the success of her lectures and newspaper articles alerted her to the budding commercialization of the sport and the fact that many people who would never attempt a high peak liked reading about someone who did. The contrivance of her accounts for newspapers and magazines stoked public interest in her ambitious assaults, secured her necessary funding, and oriented her sport toward its future. Today books, endorsements, and documentaries are routinely included in the elaborate preparations of any major expedition, and the hyping of the challenge and ordeal is ever more flagrant and imperative. For Peck at the time, the risks of such exaggeration approximated those of adverse weather, crevasses, and cliffs; she had to press bravely ahead hoping they would not undo her—and eventually they did.

THREE

Bill Reid

The Play That Changed Football

The alumni association had raised a fortune to help the football team beat its rivals. The university president perceived the team as a threat to the school's academic mission. The coach desperately wanted to win and was frantically urging his players to follow his directions and to pass their courses. Meanwhile, newspapers featured stories about injuries and how dangerous the game had become.

Sound familiar?

In this case the year was 1905. Three years before, Harvard's alumni had decided that its football team was important enough to contribute one hundred thousand dollars for construction of a grand, state-of-the-art stadium. Continuing losses to Yale spurred them to raise additional funding to hire a new coach, one of the game's first salaried professionals. Charles Eliot, arguably the most illustrious of Harvard presidents, had long supported his faculty's fruitless opposition to football, but the recent surge of money into the game, the fancy new stadium, widespread recruiting abuses, and worst of all, the mounting evidence of player injuries and deaths had infused his opposition with new fervor. And he was not alone. Thousands from all over the country, both inside and outside academia, shared his objections. If

Eliot were to forge this opposition into an organized campaign, the game might very well be abolished. On the other hand, such a victory could alienate him from his wealthy, influential alumni and turn the new stadium into a useless monstrosity.

The new coach was Bill Reid, formerly one of Harvard's finest athletes. Following graduation, he had remained a year as a graduate coach and guided the football team to one of its greatest seasons. Several years later he agreed to resume coaching at Harvard, but only after assurance of necessary financial support for him and his family. Determined to prove that his salary was justified and that his earlier success was no fluke, he concentrated on ending domination of the team by "gentleman" players from pedigreed families and developing it into a potent, cohesive unit. He ignored Eliot's complaint and focused instead on Walter Camp, the architect of Yale's indomitable football teams and longtime head of the influential Rules Committee of the Intercollegiate Football Association, which effectively determined how the game was played. Camp's years of coping with objections and mediating disagreements inclined him to hear the recent complaints about the game as nuisance echoes from the past. The incontrovertible evidence of football's popularity convinced him that fans liked the game as it was.

Luckily, Reid, football, and the cause of reform got much needed support from the other president, Theodore Roosevelt, Harvard graduate and zealous advocate of strenuous sport. Roosevelt respected Eliot as an educational leader but considered him a curmudgeon about football. Roosevelt was also sensitive enough to public opinion to realize that the mounting criticism of the game constituted a serious threat.

Thus he summoned Reid from the practice field to the White House and solicited his advice on how to breech Camp's roadblock and achieve reform. They agreed that Harvard *had* to beat Yale both on the field and in the conference room.

Unlike the other sports covered in this book, football originated as a collegiate game, and this association profoundly influenced its development. Historians consider the first game to have been a November 6, 1869, match between Rutgers and Princeton on a vast field in New Brunswick with twenty-five average-sized men on each side. A soccer ball was used, and players were not allowed to run with it or throw it; goals were scored by kicking it between pairs of posts at opposite ends of the field. Rutgers prevailed 6–4 in the first meeting, but Princeton won a rematch 8–0.[1]

Student enthusiasm for these contests proved prescient as Yale, Columbia, the University of Pennsylvania, Cornell, and Harvard soon formed teams of their own. Early matches between these schools exposed a problematic lack of agreement on rules and prompted an 1873 conference of student players to establish a uniform set. Princeton and Yale continued to favor a game resembling soccer, but Harvard preferred running the ball and did not attend the conference because it did not think compromise was possible. In 1875 the captain of the Harvard football team challenged Yale's captain to an initial meeting that effectively resolved their opposed biases. In return for Harvard coming to New Haven and several other minor concessions, Yale agreed to running with the ball and tackling. Harvard won the match and converted its rival, along with visiting observers from Princeton, to its game. Harvard's style of play was formally approved a year later by student representatives from these schools and Columbia at a Springfield meeting that created the Intercollegiate Football Association (IFA).[2]

That same fall Walter Camp entered Yale, and for the next six years—four as an undergraduate and two as a medical student—he played on Yale football teams that never lost to Harvard. During his sophomore year he became Yale's representative to the first meeting of the Rules Committee of the IFA and served on this committee until his death in 1925. At an early meeting he proposed that the number of players on each side be reduced from the current fifteen to the eleven that Yale had always favored. This change was not passed until 1880, when the committee also approved a line of scrimmage to replace the rugby-like "scrummage." This adoption ended continuous play and clearly differentiated football from rugby. When the ball carrier was downed, play stopped and did not resume until a "snapper" in the middle of a redefined offensive line booted (rather than snapped) the ball backward to a quarterback. Two years later Camp and fellow members adopted another rule, which required a team to relinquish the ball if it did not gain five yards (or if it lost ten) in three downs, a change that led to imprinting the field with "gridiron" lines five yards apart. These modifications transformed the amorphous original game into one of orderly play supervised by a referee.[3]

After dropping out of medical school and working in New York City for a year, Camp took a position with the New Haven Clock Company and reconnected with Yale football. At this time teams were coached by captains, but this dual responsibility of coaching and playing was too much of a distraction. The positions were separated, and a recently

16. Walter Camp.
(Walter Camp Papers, Manuscripts and Archives, Yale University Library)

graduated player was appointed to coach. Since Camp had been captain for three of his six years as a player and was again nearby, he began advising and instructing the team. His contributions were so helpful and so well received that his involvement gradually increased. Following his marriage in 1887, he began sending his wife to practices, deliberating over her reports, and then conferring with the team captain during evenings after work. In 1889 he was officially appointed "graduate advisor" to the football team, a position he retained until 1910, when Yale contracted its first professional coach. Since Camp's regular job limited his attendance at practices, even after he became president of his company in 1903, he enlisted graduating players to remain as "field coaches," and several went on to became successful coaches elsewhere.[4] Awkward though this arrangement was, it yielded stunning results. Yale's unbeaten teams of 1891 and 1892 prevailed over their opponents 923–0.[5]

Yale's extraordinary success escalated football's popularity. Nine years after its first match against Harvard, this rivalry had acquired enough appeal that the game was played at the Polo Grounds in New York City over Thanksgiving and drew a record ten thousand spectators.[6] The game's popularity also sparked controversy, and university faculty were among its first and most vocal critics. The faculties of both Princeton and Rutgers fretted over student interest in the very first game, and by 1883 football was perceived as so alien to the university's intellectual mission that Harvard created an Athletic Committee and had it evaluate the game. Its report decried the game's prizefight atmosphere in which players hit opponents in the face and threw them violently to the turf. Instead of condemning brutal play, partisans in the stands encouraged members of their team to "slug him," "break his neck," and "kill him." Concluding that football was "demoralizing" and "extremely dangerous," the committee urged that Harvard abolish its team, and the faculty approved the recommendation.[7] Although the football team played no games in 1885, this decision was vigorously opposed by students and alumni, and a new Athletic Committee was appointed to reconsider it. This committee proposed that the game be reinstated and justified its reversal with the frequently voiced argument that "roughness, unaccompanied by brutality and unfair play, often tends to develop courage, presence of mind, and a manly spirit."[8]

Two rule changes implemented in 1888 — one banning hands and outstretched arms for blocking and another allowing tackling below the waist — altered the prevailing style of play and rekindled opposition.[9] The first rule permitted blockers to furnish interference for the ball carrier beyond the line of scrimmage, but compelled them to use only forearms and shoulders against opponents. The second one encouraged the ball carrier to stay behind his protection and avoid the open field. As blockers clustered and defenders gathered to oppose them, encounters, which had previously pitted one player against another, became clashes between armies. These modifications inspired Harvard's famous "flying wedge" of 1892, in which lines of blockers converged from each side of the field to form a penetrating V in front of the ball carrier. This play was devised for kickoffs and used sparingly, but it garnered enormous attention because it so vividly exemplified the new concentration of play. Variations of this scheme sprang up along the line of scrimmage as blockers positioned themselves behind the line and started moving forward before the ball was snapped. By carefully timing their advance, they developed forward momentum without going off-sides. These tactics intensified collisions, making the contest at once more exciting and more dangerous.

By 1894 growing concern over the increased injuries from mass play prompted calls for rule changes, but the IFA was in disarray. Harvard had already quit the organization over Princeton's "tramp athletes," and a recent move to eliminate the eligibility of graduate students provoked Penn to withdraw as well. With Princeton and Yale the only big schools left, the Intercollegiate Football Association continued to exist in name only.[10] The ensuing season exposed the consequences of these unresolved disagreements. Early in the season, when Penn triumphed over Princeton in Trenton with two second-half scores, riots broke out afterward, and the two teams did not play each other again for forty-one years.[11] The Harvard-Yale game, held that year in Springfield, caused so many injuries that it became known as "the bloody battle of Hampton Field." After a failed score and a fumbled punt, a frustrated Harvard player bloodied the eye of a Yale tackle and set off a wave of reprisals, which peaked when Frank Hinkey, a Yale star known for his roughness, drove his knees into a Harvard player already on the ground and broke his collar bone and knee. By the end of the game, a third of the participants had sustained some kind of injury, a casualty rate, a prominent magazine noted, exceeding that of Napoleon's army at Waterloo.[12]

This brutality so upset Harvard's faculty that it rushed through a new motion to abolish the game by a two-thirds vote, and President Eliot strongly endorsed the decision.

"The game of football grows worse and worse as regards foul and violent play and the number and gravity of injuries which the players suffer," he wrote in his annual report. "It has become perfectly clear that the game as now played is unfit for college use." However, the Athletic Committee, which now consisted of three students, three alumni, and three faculty members, urged that the game be allowed to continue and referred the matter to the Board of Overseers, which affirmed its authority in disputes like this and sided with the Athletic Committee.[13] Nonetheless, Harvard canceled all athletic competitions with Yale for 1895, and the football teams did not play each other again until Camp successfully negotiated resumption of the rivalry for 1897.[14] A complementary revival of the IFA produced some new rule changes, including one that limited forward motion to a single player, but a crucial component of this revival was careful avoidance of the strains that had almost destroyed the organization.[15] Camp was so pleased with these compromises that he decided the game would be best served in the future by simply leaving it alone. As one historian has characterized this point in the game's development, "because the rule makers had helped to shape the existing game, they saw American football from the standpoint of a successful finished product and proceeded slowly in making changes."[16]

William T. Reid Jr. enrolled at Harvard in September 1897, the year that Harvard resumed its football rivalry with Yale. Though not highly regarded as a football prospect, he soon proved himself to be a superior player and went on to become a central figure in the next phase of the game's controversy. Reid grew up far from the predominant constituency of Harvard, in San Francisco, where his father was principal of Boy's High School. William Sr. was raised on a farm in Illinois and fought in the Civil War, but so wanted an education that he borrowed money to attend Harvard. After serving as a high school principal in Newport, Rhode Island, as assistant headmaster at Boston Latin School, and as superintendent of public schools in Brookline, he was offered the position of president of the University of California and relocated to Berkeley when his son was three years old. Anyone who succeeded the popular and highly respected John LeConte would have had a tough job, but a contentious search left Reid impaired before he ever started. Faculty and several members of the regents favored a popular professor, but a majority of the regents opposed his candidacy and demanded that the search include outsiders. Reid's strong recommendations from Harvard professors and President Eliot narrowed the applicant pool to himself and another candidate, who admitted that he would only serve until a more appropriate selection could be made. Reid's slim 11 to 7 margin left the regents divided and the faculty disgruntled.[17] After three futile, demoralizing years of service, Reid resigned to open a preparatory school in Belmont, south of San Francisco, which he ran until 1918.

Young Bill attended his father's school, where he excelled in baseball and football. Since Walter Camp had friends on the West Coast and even coached briefly at Stanford, he was undoubtedly aware of Bill's athletic potential, but his father's Harvard connection made recruitment for Yale a waste of time. During his freshman year in Cambridge, Bill tried out for both football and baseball. The baseball coach started him as catcher on the varsity team, and Reid lettered all four years and was the team captain his final two years. During

17. Sophomore Bill Reid, fullback, 1898.

(Harvard University Archives, HUP Reid, William, 13)

his senior year the team won all its games against Yale and went 18-2, its best record since 1868. He is among the few Harvard catchers ever to complete an errorless season, and it was mainly his baseball acclaim that prompted the *Boston Transcript*, in its announcement of his wedding, to characterize him as "one of the best athletes that ever came out [of Harvard]."[18]

Reid's performance in football was less impressive, but he played a key role in a momentous victory over Yale. He started on a freshman team blessed with exceptional talent and made the varsity the following year. Over the course of that team's undefeated, untied season, he worked his way into a starting position at fullback for the Yale game, which was held in New Haven that year. He scored both touchdowns in Harvard's glorious 17–0 triumph, only its second victory over Yale since the original 1875 contest.

Injuries curtailed Reid's play as a junior. He damaged his leg in the second game of the season and was sidelined for most of October. By the time he had healed enough to return, only two games remained and S. G. Ellis had replaced him.[19] Reid was listed as a substitute for the Yale game and saw little action in the scoreless tie, which deprived Harvard of a second perfect season. Because Ellis was a junior, Reid knew he would have to outperform him in order to regain his starting position and elected to forego football his senior year.

Although Reid played little football his final two years, he was invited to return and coach the team following his graduation. Reid's uneven performance certainly made this a surprising decision, but extenuating circumstances played a large role. The previous season the team was wracked with internal dissention, which did not manifest itself until a final 28–0 loss to Yale. Like most Ivy League teams at the time, many of the players on Harvard's squad came from elite eastern families. These "gentlemen amateurs," who could easily afford the costs of Harvard's education and its exclusive clubs, participated in football to prove that their upper-class status had diminished neither their competitiveness nor their prowess, but they also tended to favor their own and closed ranks against outsiders. Ben Dibblee, captain of the team that year, and John Hallowell, a first team All-American, came from prominent backgrounds and probably would have been selected for the coaching position over Reid had their personal and class sense of superiority not exacerbated turmoil within the team.[20] In his letters home Reid complained about Harvard's entrenched snobbery, which ranged well beyond the football team, and his father counseled him to conduct himself as though it did not exist. Bill's conscientious implementation of this advice and his unpretentiousness so impressed his classmates that they elected him to be one of the two class marshalls.[21] Nonetheless, Reid's objections to elitism on the team were as much a factor in his decision not to play football his senior year as his injury. Moreover, he harbored a hostility toward privilege that would persist and develop into a stern self-righteousness about his own fairness. That is to say, Reid's selection as coach owed more to his distance from the team's current problems, his fervent egalitarianism, and his enormous popularity than any special or proven understanding of football. In a later reflection on his coaching, a Harvard dean would write, "Your standing for democracy and ridding every man of the feeling that want of social position could be counted against him in athletics is one of your great services."[22]

Reid swiftly demonstrated that he was the coach Harvard needed. His team completed the 1901 season untied and undefeated. After crushing its first nine opponents 232–24, it routed Yale 22–0 before thirty-six thousand euphoric fans who deliriously celebrated Yale's first defeat in Cambridge. The ensuing spring Reid coached baseball, and his team lost only three of its twenty-four games. He financed this additional year with a fellowship for working on a master's degree and serving as proctor of a residence hall. While Reid concentrated on coaching and his studies, his fiancée and her family went on an extended trip to Europe.[23] In July, following their reunion, they were married. In order to provide for his young new wife and their plans for children, Reid quit coaching and returned to California to teach at his father's prep school.

The 1898 and 1901 football triumphs over Yale inspired Harvard fans to hope for more outstanding teams and better accommodation. Maj. Henry Lee Higginson, a Civil War veteran and successful head of a Boston brokerage firm, had donated a tract of undeveloped land for Harvard sports. Believing that the football team deserved a larger and more imposing facility, the twenty-fifth reunion of the class of '79 emulated Higginson's example and raised one hundred thousand dollars for a new stadium with capacity for thirty-five thousand. The renowned New York architectural firm of McKim, Mead, and White was enlisted to plan a modern, steel-reinforced concrete structure and to design it as an open-ended Greco-Roman amphitheater.[24] Unfortunately, Dartmouth spoiled its opening in the fall of 1903 by winning 11–0, and Yale sparked fear that the stadium might be jinxed when it thrashed Harvard 16–0 two weeks later.

18. Yale game at Harvard Stadium, 1905.
(Library of Congress, LC-USZ62-125359)

The $100,000 gift from the class of '79 was less than half of the whopping $220,000-plus cost of this stadium, and the Athletic Committee agreed to cover the rest. Over the 1890s, the ever-increasing popularity of football generated so much money that the Athletic Committee took control of finances away from students. By 1903 the committee had accumulated enough assets to contribute $50,000 toward the stadium and to assume a mortgage for the rest. Ira Hollis, chair of both the Athletic Committee and the engineering department, used these contributions as leverage to involve members from his department in the project.[25] Over the fall of 1904, the football team rewarded this investment with a profit of $51,232.[26]

The new stadium, the recent losses, and this potent revenue stream moved the Athletic Committee to intrude itself, albeit cautiously, upon the tradition of the football captain

selecting the team's coach. After an enlarged search with input from the team, the position was offered to Edgar Wrightington, the player hurt by Hinkey in the infamous "bloody battle of Hampton Field." The current captain of the football team had recommended Reid and urged that he be offered a salary, but the Athletic Committee was unwilling to breech the longstanding policy that football, as collegiate sport, was emphatically for amateurs and should be free of all professionalism. Reid had responded positively to the committee's initial inquiry about his availability, but explained that he and his young family could not afford to give up his current salary. "It is one of the hardest things I've ever done, to force myself to write one word about the pecuniary side of this question," he confessed. "I feel as though I could never do enough for Harvard, and it seems ungrateful, almost to have to hold out any conditions whatever."[27]

When Wrightington's team went 7-3-1 and lost again to Yale, he stepped down. This resignation, the expanded responsibilities of the coach, and the few qualified replacements willing to serve without compensation convinced the Athletic Committee to amend its search plans and tap its ample funding. "What we all desire is undoubtedly amateur coaching," its new chair announced to the press, but "the evidence which now comes to the committee from all sides seems to be in favor of a paid coach."[28] Four months later, under a headline proclaiming "Princely Salary to Coach," the *New York Times* announced that Reid had accepted the coaching position and a salary of $3,500. The article that followed revealed that the committee had worried that Reid's compensation nearly matched that of full professors and purposely chose a lower figure.[29] However, without public announcement the Athletic Association of Harvard Graduates agreed to match the stipend from the Athletic Committee. These two sums raised Reid's salary almost to that of President Eliot.[30] Reid was not the first professional coach in football, but he was at the forefront of a developing trend. Following Columbia's victory over Yale in 1902, George Foster had his salary raised to $5,000, and the same year that Reid returned to Harvard, Alonzo Stagg requested and received $6,000 to coach football at the University of Chicago.[31]

The Athletic Committee's pursuit of Reid and its approval of his grand salary were rooted in a conviction that he was uniquely qualified to produce a team worthy of Harvard's new stadium. The conscientiousness with which Reid shouldered his responsibilities as coach is reflected in the more than fifteen hundred typewritten pages of notes he amassed over the brief two years he filled the position. These journals reveal that one of Reid's foremost concerns was to turn his players into serious students. He monitored their class performance, established a program of academic tutoring, and hoped that these procedures would signal to the faculty his respect for their authority. He confided to himself at one point, "The matter of following men upon their studies has been one of the most trying that I've had during the whole time."[32]

Reid also devised a weight-training program and created a special meal table for his players. He prepared a card catalog in which he noted the height and weight of *every* Harvard student with an eye to the position he might be able to play. Reid explored ways to improve equipment to avoid injuries and sought better techniques for treating them. He developed a network of alumni and prep schools for locating promising talent and crafted a schedule that gave his team an opportunity to develop before it faced stiff competition.[33]

Finally, Reid recruited a dozen assistants, one for each player position. These included Percy Haughton, who was responsible for kicking. He would go on to become one of Harvard's most successful coaches and train Charles Brinkley, the greatest of all drop-kickers. Reid selected William Lewis to be his chief assistant.[34] Lewis, an African American, had gone from rural Virginia to Amherst, where he played football for four years. When he enrolled in Harvard Law School, existing eligibility rules allowed him to continue playing. As center he made first team on Camp's All-American list for 1892 and 1893 and participated in the first use of the flying wedge.[35] After graduation he elected to practice law in the Boston area so that he could continue helping the football team. His contribution to the triumphant 1898 season so impressed Reid that he had Lewis join him when he became coach in 1901 and negotiated a $500 stipend for him. Along with a raise to $1,000 for the 1905 season, Reid awarded Lewis responsibility for linemen and defense and used him as a centerpiece for social change. Reid later explained that, when he returned to Cambridge, morale was dismal and team members did not speak to one another when they passed on their way to class.[36] Reid was so intent on correcting this problem that he told the Athletic Committee that he was prepared "to put a colored fellow, a Chinaman or a South African native in, if he was the best man."[37] He conceived of Lewis as linchpin support for these words. "I regard Lewis," he explained, "as one of the most valuable and able fellows and one of the easiest to work with, which is a great point."[38]

Reid took the practice field determined to produce a winning football team—over Yale, above all. Reforming football was not on his long list of things to do, but an early warning of trouble ahead emerged from renewed objection to football from Harvard's president. Eliot was outraged that the class of '79 had raised so much money for the new stadium and blithely ignored Harvard's educational needs. "How long the Stadium may endure is an open question," he fulminated. "But while it stands it will remain a conspicuous evidence of the fact that twenty five years ago Harvard taught its students to care for nothing so much as for athletic sports." He also pointed out that the university budget, which he controlled, did not contribute a single dollar toward construction of the stadium. The fact that Reid's new salary almost matched his probably aggravated this dyspepsia. His annual report for 1903–4, released early in 1905, featured an extended attack on football, which he allowed a prominent magazine to quote at length and subsequently published in the college alumni magazine under the title

"The Evils of Football." Though his denunciations of the game's brutality echoed familiar complaints about football, he singled out a glaring perversity in its existing rules that would soon prove eerily prescient: "To strike a player with clenched fists is unnecessary roughness; to give him a blow equally severe with the base of the open hand is not unnecessary roughness."[39]

Over the summer Eliot's complaints gained potent support from two exposés in influential journals. *Outlook*, which also published excerpts from Eliot's annual report and several proposals for reforming football, ran a July article titled "The Money Power in College Athletics." Its author, Clarence Deming, a former captain of Yale's baseball team, furnished a wealth of information on Yale's athletic budget and presented it as a worrisome trend. He revealed that back in 1892–93 the college's athletic programs were already grossing receipts of $51,292 and a profit of $6,084, and that these figures had swollen to $106,396 and $16,586 by the past year. Accumulated profits in a "fund of large but indefinite amount" were squirreled away for "future athletic emergencies." Although Deming reassured his readers that the unidentified controllers of this money (mainly Camp) were "responsible and competent," he expressed concern that this "atmosphere of wealth" encouraged "the mercenary spirit, the wastage, and the luxury which are in all respects bad."[40]

This close financial accounting and vague generalizations about their consequences received compelling support and clarification from a two-part investigation of college athletics by Henry Beach Needham, one into "recruiting and subsidizing" and the other on "amateur code; its evasion and administration." *McClure's* magazine, which ran these

articles, was already well known for its muckraking exposés
of political and corporate corruption, and this examination
of collegiate sport found practices as scandalous as those
of big business. Colleges were locked in a ruinous competition to secure the best athletes. A Princeton recruiter was
combing prep schools for promising talent and shepherd-
ing his best finds through exams and entrance applications.
The University of Pennsylvania was an outright thief, first
beating Penn State over the weekend and then adding one
of its best players to its roster the following week. A sig-
nificant amount of Yale's success on the gridiron was due
to its successful evasion of the collegiate code that players
be amateurs. James Hogan, All-American tackle and captain of the 1904 team, received luxurious accommodations,
special meals, and a ten-day vacation in Cuba, along with
commissions from sales of cigarettes around the campus and
scorecards at home games. According to Needham football
was generating so much money that abuses like these were
commonplace and unstoppable. Harvard's new stadium
was presented as a prime example of this "glorification of
gate money," and Professor Hollis, chairman of the Athletic
Committee, which approved its construction, confessed, "If
I had it to do over again, realizing its cost, I should not con-
sent to its construction."[41]

Theodore Roosevelt knew Needham, and after he read
these articles, he conferred with the journalist to learn more.
Meanwhile, Endicott Peabody, headmaster of the prep
school that Roosevelt's son had attended and leader of a
group of concerned administrators, urged Roosevelt to convene representatives from the Big Three—Harvard, Yale,
and Princeton—and get them to agree "to play football

19. Mass play in Harvard football game, 1902.
(Harvard University Archives, HUPSF Football, 56)

honestly." Roosevelt, who favored use of his position as a "bully pulpit," liked Peabody's suggestion and chose to host an October meeting in Washington DC, even though the football season was already under way by this point.[42]

At the time Reid was preoccupied with his team. With solid victories in the first two games of his carefully planned schedule and a more difficult one looming, he preferred to remain at practice and not travel to the White House, but he realized that a presidential invitation was not a choice. During the October 9 luncheon, Roosevelt mentioned the mounting concern over unfair play, cited instances in which players were encouraged to evade the rules, and invited feedback. Reid recorded in his diary that Camp actively participated but "was very slippery and did not allow himself to be pinned down to anything." Both he and the representatives from Princeton respectfully denied fostering injurious play. At the end of the meeting, the president requested that his guests draft a public declaration of accord, and they complied with a terse statement declaring their agreement "to carry out in letter and in spirit the rules of the game of foot ball relating to roughness, holding, and foul play."[43]

If Roosevelt's intervention had the unanticipated effect of giving legitimacy to the recent criticism of football, as one football historian has aptly observed, it also narrowed the problem to the familiar one of the game's brutality and marginalized the recent complaints about monetary excesses and recruiting abuses.[44] Reid's notes on his Washington trip also reveal that the group's proclaimed accord lacked meaningful agreement. Hoping to capitalize on the press release and achieve some specific improvements during the return train trip, Reid pointed out the lack of definition in the current rule on unnecessary roughness, proposed a supplementary list of specific infractions, and sought group approval for a few of them. But the conversation went nowhere. "I must say, that I do not feel that Yale and Princeton were wholly in sympathy with the idea, although they professed to be," he reflected afterward. He then added, "I think a good stiff official would do more in regard to this matter than anything else."[45]

All six representatives realized that it was easier and more expedient to support the "spirit of rules" than to agree on specific violations. Ronald Smith, the foremost authority on early collegiate sport, has perceptively observed, "In England, there was an upper-class understanding in rugby, as in other sports, that the spirit of the rules was as important as the rules themselves. In America, the letter of the rules might

be observed, but the spirit of the rules was much underval-
ued."[46] Although American conversion of the loose game of
rugby into the more orderly game of football necessitated
creation and approval of specific rules, the ongoing resistance to further change from Camp and the IFA breathed
new life into the previously unworkable "spirit of the rules"
as a base of agreement that extinguished the need for change
and better definition. Because Roosevelt and the general
public understood and still respected this venerable ideal, the
six college representatives successfully invoked it to satisfy
the president's charge. But when Reid offered his addendum
of suggestions and got nowhere, he sensed that this approval
for the "spirit" was, in fact, an avoidance of potentially fractious debate. It was also invested with a vain hope that this
accord would check the clamor for reform until the end of
the season.

Reid's alternative hope for "a good stiff official" inad-
equately considered the enormous responsibility he was
delegating.

The month following the meeting at the White House was
for Reid tense and trying. His young, talented team continued to win, and everyone realized that the upcoming Penn
game in Philadelphia would be a momentous test of the two
undefeated teams. All of Reid's careful preparation was upended early in the game when he discovered that the areas
inside the 25-yard lines had been heavily watered the night
before and that Penn's players were wearing special cleats
for these conditions. Over the first half, Harvard outrushed
Penn 160 yards to 10, but its drives stalled in the boggy sec-
tions of the field and a fumble near the 10-yard line enabled
Penn to take a 6–0 lead. Harvard scored in the second half,

but the team wore out and lost 12–6. The players were so demoralized that Reid shouldered blame for the loss and announced that his poor coaching had let everyone down.[47]

The toll of this setback on Reid was worsened by persisting opposition to football. On Wednesday before the Penn game, Reid learned that President Eliot was secretly lobbying Harvard's Board of Overseers to abolish the game. Reid, Lewis, Herbert White, and William Sullivan, a Harvard alum and sportswriter for the *Boston Globe*, sought to defuse this threat with a letter, signed by Reid, which echoed familiar Eliot complaints and argued for an alternative objective. "I have become convinced that the game as it is played to-day has fundamental faults which cannot be removed by any mere technical revision of the rules," he asserted. "The game ought to be radically changed." The letter itself went to the Athletic Association of Harvard Graduates, and Sullivan posted copies to the leading newspapers of New England and New York.[48]

Following a dispiriting tie with Dartmouth, Reid looked forward to the Yale game in Cambridge as a final vindication. But it was not to be. Several days beforehand, newspapers ominously reported that Dan Hurley, captain of the Harvard team, was hospitalized with a blood clot on the brain sustained in the previous game.[49] This storm cloud darkened over the game's scoreless first half and even tenser second half, in which neither team was able to move the ball. Finally, with only five minutes left, a Harvard player disobeyed Reid's instructions, fielded a punt, and turned the ball over deep in his own territory. Yale capitalized, pushed across the only score of the game, and won 6–0.

This stunning defeat devastated everyone associated with

Harvard and brought special significance to an initially minor incident from the first half. As soon as Harvard All-American "Hooks" Burr fielded a punt, he was immediately struck high and low by two Yale tacklers. James Quill, the one who came high, struck Burr in the face with outstretched arms and broke his nose, which bled profusely, but no penalty was called.

Had Harvard won, Burr's catch would have remained a trivial moment, merely another play. Since he did not fumble the ball and continued to play, the *Harvard Crimson* and the *New York Times* did not even mention the play in their accounts of the game.[50] The *Harvard Bulletin*, a weekly journal for alumni, offered the longest, most detailed report on the game and noted only that Burr "attempted a fair catch" and was downed by a blow to the nose.[51] However, the same issue also contained a hastily included editorial titled "Roughness in Football," which denounced Quill's blow as a glaring example of all that wrong with football. After maintaining that Burr had signaled for a fair catch, the unnamed author reported that at least twenty spectators had reported to him that Burr had been hit in the face with a closed fist, and he harshly condemned the official, Paul Dashiell, for failing to call unnecessary roughness:

> Much of the recent criticism of football has been due to the inefficiency of the officials. . . . We have no desire to say any unkind things about anyone, but we believe that Dashiell more than anyone else is responsible for the fact that the spirit of the rules has not been carried out. He has acted as umpire in many of the games of recent years, but he has never done more than enforce the letter of the law.

20. Paul J. Dashiell.
(Special Collections and Archives Department,
Nimitz Library, United States Naval Academy)

We do not recall when he has disqualified a player in an important game because the latter was guilty of unnecessary roughness, and yet instances when he should have done so can be told by the dozen. . . . There can be no doubt that Quill's attack on Burr was rough; it is equally true that it was unnecessary. Why then should Quill not have been disqualified?[52]

With over twenty years of experience, Paul J. Dashiell had refereed six previous Harvard-Yale games and ten consecutive Yale-Princeton games and been a member of the IFA's Rules Committee since 1894. For the past two seasons he had coached Navy's football team and successfully reversed its long string of ignominious defeats with a 1905 finish of ten wins, one loss, and one tie, a record unsurpassed until 1926.[53] Certainly he possessed formidable qualifications for his position and was indeed "a good stiff official" in ruling against the expectations of the rabidly partisan, home team crowd.

The Sunday edition of the *Boston Globe* was the only article on the game to give the Quill blow more than passing mention, and its coverage furnished the inspiration for the *Bulletin*'s hurried editorial. For the many Harvard fans in its readership and as support for its commitment to reform of the game, the *Globe* ran two accounts of the game that started on the newspaper's front page and were positioned so that they framed a centerpiece photograph of Burr making his catch. If these two accounts sparked the long-standing infamy of this play, they also provide crucial information that *was* quickly forgotten. They reveal that there were two other officials on the field and that existing rules supported

Dashiell's controversial decision. As the umpire, Dashiell was the final authority, but his call was based on input from Edgar Whiting, a linesman, and Thomas Lee "Bum" Mc-Clung, a referee, who was closest to the incident.[54] The photograph of Burr's disputed catch shows McClung fewer than ten feet away and well positioned to judge what actually happened. Amazingly enough for us today, a receiver at this time was expected to signal a fair catch by denting the turf with his heel.[55] Eliot himself had already called attention to another perversity in the existing rules whereby a closed-fist blow was an infraction warranting a penalty but one with the heel of an open hand was not—a distinction Quill certainly understood. Dashiell, anyone on the sidelines, and especially spectators in the stands would have had great difficulty discerning the crucial intricacies of Burr's foot movement and Quill's blow. From his immediate proximity, McClung checked that Burr did *not* "heel" the turf and determined that he was struck with an open hand rather than a closed fist.[56] In his account W. T. Sullivan, the Harvard alumnus who had helped Reid with his earlier public letter on the football situation, noted that Dashiell conferred with McClung (and perhaps Whiting) before deciding that no infraction had occurred. In "a long talk" following the game, Sullivan learned from Dashiell that McClung's judgment on the fair catch made everything that followed "perfectly legitimate play allowed by the rules."[57] In other words, Dashiell's call involved both crucial information from another official and a thorough knowledge of the pertinent rules.

Nonetheless, Dashiell's explanation did not prevent Sullivan from writing, "It was certainly an instance of unnecessary roughness and the rules distinctly allow the umpire to inflict a penalty for unnecessary roughness."[58] The alumni editorial, which faulted Dashiell for not calling unnecessary roughness, did not consider that he and fellow officials believed that football was a rough game and that "unnecessary" roughness was an inherently subjective call; they preferred to base their decisions on rules with sharper definition.

In the locker room prior to the game, Reid had a testy dispute over the distinction between specific, defined rules and their "spirit" with John Owsley, a Yale coach. Reid maintained that Yale players were illegally locking each other's legs to wall out opponents. When Owsley pointed out that the actual wording of the rules did not forbid this tactic, Reid countered that "the spirit of rules" did and argued that decisions on this objectionable practice ought "to be left to the officials." As Dashiell and McClung stood by listening, Owsley shot back, "Well, if you want to undertake to interpret the rules and forbid something the rules allow, of course that is your privilege, but it is something I would not care to do if I were an official."[59] How much this exchange influenced the controversial decision on Burr is impossible to say, but Reid was so upset over Dashiell's call that he actively and successfully conspired to terminate his career as an official.[60]

A third column, to the left of the *Globe*'s two front-page accounts of the game, informed readers that Harold Moore, a halfback for Union College, had died from injuries sustained in another game that same day. This account revealed that when Henry MacCracken, the chancellor of New York University, learned of Moore's death, he immediately dispatched a telegram to President Eliot urging him to convene college presidents for serious discussion on the future of football. The following day the *Globe* reported that over the past season, 19 football players had been killed and 137 had been seriously injured.[61] Even though Eliot declined Mac-Cracken's request and urged everyone to allow the situation to cool before taking any action, Columbia's president and faculty hurried through a vote to disband its team.

At this point the pressures and demands of the previous season had sorely strained Reid's health. Back in 1904 he had replied to the Athletic Committee's initial overture, "I am of a very nervous temperament and very addicted to worrying . . . and I don't quite know whether I could last a good stiff campaign or not."[62] Less than a month into his 1905 schedule, Reid noticed that he had already lost six pounds and vowed not to repeat his 1901 experience when he had "worried [himself] into a state of practical uselessness." But by the end of October, he confessed, "I am badly over[s] trained I know and while I struggle against it as hard as I can, I have not got enough vitality to struggle sufficiently. I simply go around in the morning so nervous that I am unable to apply myself to anything." Late in the season the team doctor was so concerned about Reid's deteriorating health that he slipped sedatives into his drink to help him sleep.[63]

But the tsunami set off by Quill's blow and the death of Moore compelled Reid to postpone the recuperation he acutely needed. In early December President Roosevelt summoned him again to Washington, this time "for the purpose of going over the [football] situation in the light of recent developments."[64] When Reid arrived at the White House, Roosevelt explained that many Harvard graduates had contacted him about the Burr incident, and he asked Reid for a full accounting. Reid maintained that Dashiell had indeed mishandled the call. He also admitted that he had given up on "spirit of the rules" and was now totally convinced that radical reform was imperative. The only way to achieve better officiating was to equip referees with better, more explicit rules. As Reid later claimed (and the Burr incident had already demonstrated), the existing rules were "a mass of incongruities and contradictions."[65]

Reid also explained that MacCracken's call for action was gathering momentum despite the refusal of the Big Three to participate. The New York University chancellor had organized a major meeting, scheduled for three days hence, and received commitments from thirteen institutions. This gathering would produce an 8–5 vote in favor of reform and an agreement to convene again to formulate strategies for achieving it on December 28, a date chosen because it immediately preceded an already-scheduled meeting of the Rules Committee of the IFA.[66]

Reid's greatest concern was Walter Camp's adamant opposition to reform and the power of his influence over the IFA's committee.[67] The coach added that Dashiell owed his current position on the IFA Rules Committee to Camp's influence. Reid then explained that this stacked deck had dealt them a powerful trump card. Dashiell, whose main appointment at the Naval Academy was that of a chemistry instructor, had divulged to Reid that he was under consideration for a major promotion, that "this promotion was the ambition of his life," and that he was hoping Reid could persuade Roosevelt to support it.[68] Reid proposed that Roosevelt instead delay the promotion until Dashiell converted to the side of rule reform.

Once he and Roosevelt had roughed out this strategy, Reid incurred the daunting task of preparing sweeping rule changes for the upcoming IFA meeting. Despite his exhaustion, he; Lewis, his African American assistant; and colleagues from Harvard's athletic staff, along with the college dean LeBaron Briggs, agreed to serve on a committee that met eleven times during December and early January, each meeting lasting four to eight hours; one was convened on Christmas day.[69]

Reid attended the December 29 meeting of the IFA Rules Committee intending to delay any motion for reform because his committee had still not completed its deliberations, but an unexpected request from MacCracken's group made this unnecessary. Its gathering the day before was attended by sixty-eight college representatives, and nine hours of acrimonious debate had produced both a new Rules Committee and a proposal to the IFA to accept an amalgamation of the two committees. Unwilling to vote immediately on such a radical initiative, the IFA's committee requested more time to confer with their institutions and scheduled a January 12 meeting for their response.[70]

The Burr controversy, the death of the Union College player, Roosevelt's personal espousal of reform, and MacCracken's flourishing initiative empowered Eliot to deliver the final component that enabled the developing plan to succeed. Twice over the fall he had presented Harvard's Board of Overseers a motion to abolish football, and both times the vote was postponed.[71] Reid's public letter on behalf of radical reform undoubtedly influenced one of these delays. However, with advance information on the nineteen rule modifications agreed upon by Reid's committee and awareness of the looming IFA meeting on January 12, Eliot convinced the Overseers to vote two days beforehand to abolish football at

Harvard—*unless* radical rule reforms were approved and implemented.[72]

Harvard, of course, had previously abolished football and then reneged, but its new stadium, its substantial mortgage, and the vastly enlarged base of fans made the risks this time much greater. Thus the Board of Overseers carefully plotted for its momentous decision to succeed.[73] Reid had to achieve reform or lose his job. Letters from Roosevelt pressured Dashiell into the equally tense position of supporting Reid or forfeiting his promotion.[74] Harvard's Athletic Committee anticipated that Camp would resist the pressure being applied and thus instructed Reid to explain that these misgivings compelled him to quit the IFA's Rules Committee and to affiliate with the new one of the Mac-Cracken group; this radical action was necessitated by the Overseers' grave mandate. From this new affiliation along with Dashiell's covert backing, Reid campaigned for a consolidation of both organizations. The success of this merger originated a new organization that became the National Collegiate Athletic Association (NCAA).[75] Reid ministered the consequential marriage of the two rules committees so that he became secretary of the amalgamated result, thereby appropriating the original basis of Camp's power and enabling him to put forward his carefully prepared slate of nineteen changes.[76]

In multiple meetings extending into April, this new committee deliberated and approved new rules that successfully convinced the Overseers to rescind their abolition of football. These included the establishment of a "neutral zone" between the offensive and defensive lines, a momentous modification that Reid credited to Lewis.[77] The offense now

21. New fair catch signal, 1906.
(Harvard University Archives, HUD 10906)

had to keep at least six men on the line of scrimmage and to make ten yards (rather than five) in three downs in order to retain the ball. The forward pass was legalized, though the revolutionary impact of this modification was delayed by imposition of a penalty for an incompletion. Other major changes included the addition of another referee, banning of open-handed blows like Quill's, and a new fair catch signal.[78]

As the architect of these reforms and secretary of the new Rules Committee, Reid assumed responsibility for writing up these changes for Spalding's official rule book for football. Ironically, Camp, who for years had been credited as the author, continued to be. In his determination to ensure that these innovations be as clear as possible, Reid supplemented the written rules with illustrative photographs (later changed into drawings), which included ones exhibiting both illegal use of the hands and the new fair catch signal. Reid later explained that he posed Harvard players for these photographs in order to "prevent another Burr incident" and to block "Yale from ever again trying to circumvent the rules."[79]

By May, when these changes were formally approved, Reid was no longer the energetic young coach of the fall before. Although the success of his team and his efforts on behalf of reform won him enormous respect and an invitation to coach the upcoming season, he suffered a devastating betrayal. Craftily, Reid had sought to limit reform to play itself, because he had much more at stake in other areas of the controversy. His strategy for the upcoming 1906 season was premised on Harvard's prestigious graduate programs and the fact that graduate students remained eligible if they had not yet completed four years of play. Having long fought upper-class domination of the football team and sought the best players without regard for their social status, Reid concluded that these were the older students enrolled in graduate school. However, this crafty plan was undone when Professor Herbert H. White, chair of the Athletic Committee, yielded to pressure from the faculty and, without informing Reid, negotiated an agreement with Yale that abolished graduate student eligibility. This left Reid with a banned wealth of talent. "I would have fielded an unbeatable team in 1906," he later explained. "It would have been a man's team, not one of college boys. . . . I had at least six men all lined up for 1906 who were twenty five to thirty years old, hard fighters all and men who loved the game. They were just the type for the old mass play and then bingo, they were eliminated."[80] This crushing setback was worsened when Reid still managed to field a powerhouse team that went undefeated until the final Yale game, which Harvard again lost 6–0 on a muffed punt.

During the eventful spring before, Dashiell and Reid crossed paths at a commemorative banquet. After dessert Dashiell broke out a box of cigars, offered the first one to Reid, and whispered into his ear, "Let's bury the hatchet."[81] Reid does not mention what he said, if anything, but he does say that he shook hands and never saw Dashiell again. A year later both Reid and Dashiell were done with football. Dashiell's promotion to full professor was approved in February, and he wrote Roosevelt a note of gratitude for supporting it. He withdrew from officiating, and that fall his football team lost only a single game and tied Army. His obituary noted that his retirement from coaching after the 1906 season was "voluntary" and that he finished his career as a professor of chemistry at the Naval Academy.[82] At the end of that same season, Reid left for California to teach again at his father's school. He eventually returned to Boston and to a successful but unfulfilling career as a bond salesman.[83] In his twenty-fifth class report, he noted his two losses to Yale, the near abolition of football, and the decimation of his graduate student plans and declared, "I looked upon the two years as a failure."[84] The passage of time eventually softened his bitterness and yielded this more balanced appraisal of his two years as Harvard's coach: "To me after all the mess I'd been through with the Graduate Rule, the revolutionary changes in the game itself, and the wrecking of my 1906 plans, this [slate of rule changes] was one achievement . . . , which gave me some satisfaction as a recompense, influencing as it did the whole future development of the game and in all probability saving the very life of the game itself."[85]

FOUR

May Sutton

California's Intrusion on Women's Tennis

The late August 1911 tournament at Niagara-on-the-Lake was an unlikely occasion for a momentous reckoning in women's tennis. This resort area on the Canadian side of the falls was not a major tennis venue. The Queen's Royal Hotel, which had hosted the event for years, always billed it as an international competition, but most of the participants came from nearby states and provinces. Since the tournament of 1911 was the twenty-fifth, organizers made a special effort to recruit premiere players in order to celebrate its silver anniversary. Hazel Hotchkiss, who had twice won the singles title at the National Championships of the U.S. National Lawn Tennis Association (currently the U.S. Open), had agreed months before to defend her titles and to play Niagara afterward. The belated decision of May Sutton likewise to compete at Niagara was a fortuitous surprise that intensified spectator interest since Sutton had not been east for several years and this would be the first time that the two players faced each other outside of California.

Sutton, an early prodigy of women's tennis, was a major contributor to the sport's transformation from a genteel game into serious competition. At seventeen she traveled to the Philadelphia Cricket Club for the National

Championships of 1904 and emerged its youngest champion until Tracy Austin claimed this distinction in 1979. The following year she sailed for England, became the first American woman to win Wimbledon, and did so again two years later. These successes established her as *the* dominant player in women's tennis but dried up funding for her to defend these titles.

Meanwhile, Hazel Hotchkiss emerged from northern California and quickly proved herself a formidable adversary. Her arsenal of diversified shots emulating men's play would alter women's tennis as much as May's competitive intensity and overpowering forehand already had. Although Sutton easily dominated their early meetings, Hotchkiss exhibited enough talent and progress for her father to fund her to compete in the National Championships. Her triumphs there and Sutton's financial constraints forced May to challenge Hazel at local tournaments, and their razor-close matches exposed differences in their personalities as pronounced as their styles of play. Hotchkiss's third triumph at the National Championships spurred Sutton to prove that she remained the superior player, and their confrontation at Niagara produced *the* most amazing one of their epic matches.

Adolphus Sutton, May's English father, entered the Royal Navy at fifteen and retired in 1890 at the age of fifty-four with the rank of captain, after fighting in the Crimean War and serving as staff commander aboard the HMS *Asia*. For several years he was harbormaster in Plymouth, where May was born on September 25, 1886—thirteen years after Maj. Walter C. Wingfield devised the game of tennis, eleven years after construction of the first courts at the All England Croquet and Lawn Tennis Club in Wimbledon, and five years

23. May, Ethel, and Florence Sutton, ca. 1910.

(Gordon Sabine)

after the National Championships in tennis for women were first held at the Casino in Newport, Rhode Island. Severe asthma convinced Adolphus to immigrate with his family in 1890 to the United States and to purchase a ten-acre ranch in California. Although he was seeking a temperate climate for his health, he chose Pasadena because English friends had settled there. His pension yielded only a modest income, but he had space for a dirt tennis court, and neighbors volunteered to help him build it. The new court inspired May and her three older sisters to play, and they rapidly developed into skillful players.[1]

When May reached ten, her older sisters, Ethel (15), Violet (14), and Florence (13), were already competing in tournaments around Los Angeles.[2] The April event at Ojai Valley was not far from Pasadena. Other competitions were held at upscale hotels in Long Beach and Newport, which used them as promotion for their recreational facilities. Once the Suttons started to win, the drive to the Coronado tournament near San Diego did not seem so far. Soon they were participating in the Pacific States Championships, the premiere West Coast event. The year-round warmth of Southern California's weather, which contributed greatly to the early popularity of tennis there, likewise encouraged this proliferation of tournaments. In addition to fostering competition, these tournaments offered diversified venues, opponents, and advisors that greatly facilitated the improvement of talented players, especially ones like the Suttons who could not have afforded them otherwise.

In 1897 Violet lost the final round of singles at the Pacific States to Marion Jones, the first woman from California to compete in the National Championships, which she won in

1899. Her trips to the East eliminated Violet's most dangerous opponent and allowed her to win the Pacific States in
1899 and 1900.[3] These victories served notice that she and
her sisters were about to dominate the event.

May played her first tournament when she was eleven.
At the time Adolphus believed she was too young for major
competition, but others argued that she was almost as good
as her sisters and he allowed her to enter the 1899 Southern
California Championships. Her first match was against her
sister Ethel, and she proceeded to win the opening set, her
first against Ethel. Her older sister immediately registered
this cold-water, wake-up call and proceeded to thrash her. In
the next round Ethel lost to Violet, who advanced to the finals, where she bested Florence. These public confrontations
intensified May's desire to play and to win. "I became most
awfully fond of it [tennis]," she reflected later, "and wanted
to be playing all the time." Though she was only fourteen
at the time of the 1901 Pacific States Championships, she
battled to the finals and took the title away from Violet. That
year doubles for women was held for the first time, and May
teamed up with Violet to win this event as well.[4] As the Sutton sisters claimed the top brackets of these competitions, a
journalist remarked, "It takes a Sutton to beat a Sutton."[5]
The phrase quickly turned into a family motto, one the Wil-
liams sisters would later revive.

After May retained her Pacific States titles through three
more tournaments, Adolphus decided that she was ready
for the National Championships but needed contributions
from neighbors to cover May's expenses. May arrived at the
Philadelphia Cricket Club expecting the players there to be
better than those in California, but she discovered that they

cared more about their gown-like attire than the score. Up to this point tennis in the East had been a decidedly upper-class sport imbued with English decorum and played on manicured grass courts at exclusive clubs. Women thought of themselves as a decidedly more feminine version of the "gentleman amateur" and approached the game as an invigorating alternative to croquet. Their goal was to look attractive, exhibit grace, and socialize. Into these exclusive, well-mannered preserves, May intruded an eye-opening determination and formidable skills honed on the fast, hard courts of California.[6] She played to WIN and was all business during her matches. As she once characterized her game, "I always played for all I was worth." Explaining how even her sisters lacked her cut-throat resolve, she observed that Ethel possessed the most versatile game but was "too good-natured."[7] May adhered to the back-and-forth baseline play favored by most women, but unlike them she raced to the ball and then drove it as hard as she could. "When you do practice[,] play for all you are worth and hard all the time," May advised in an article on improving women's play. "In practice games always try to win."[8]

May was a stocky 5 feet 4 inches and 150 pounds, and her trademark was a powerful forehand, which she deployed to intimidate and overwhelm her opponents. The aggressiveness in her play bespoke an aversion for the conventions of femininity, which, in turn, led her to advocate practical attire. "When you are on the court," she asserted in an article titled "Women and Dress," "think of your game alone and not of how you look."[9] Even as young girls, she and her sisters eschewed the popular, wide-brimmed hats and favored head bands, which were much cooler and equally effective at

24. May Sutton's powerful forehand, ca. 1910.

(Gordon Sabine)

keeping hair away from their faces. During her first appearance at Wimbledon, May, in typical fashion, hiked up her dress and rolled up her sleeves in preparation for an important point and so offended her opponent that she appealed to the referee, who made May redo her dress before play resumed.[10] After one of her many visits to Newport, May complained, "Most of the smart set there dress too elaborately for ordinary affairs and make up too much. Why, the women I played tennis with made me laugh. You would have thought they were going to a tea party. They wore picture hats tied down with fluffy veils and dainty kid gloves. They can't forget their clothes, even in athletics."[11]

May's lust for victory and athletic play enabled her to breeze through three preliminary matches of the 1904 National Championships.[12] In the finals she faced Bessie Moore, a New Yorker who had reached the finals when she was only sixteen and won the event in 1896, 1901, and 1903. She was the experienced favorite facing the precocious newcomer hoping to become the youngest champion ever. Nonetheless, Moore fared little better than Sutton's previous opponents, losing 1–6, 2–6. The *New York Times* reported that May "was marvelous and played with a confidence born of her superior ability."[13] On her return home she paused to win the Western Championships in Chicago, and her multiple opponents took a combined total of three games from her. A newspaper there reported: "In the five years she has been playing, Miss Sutton has never lost a set in tournament play."[14]

In 1905 Sutton elected to play Wimbledon. Since her parents were from England, this decision was both understandable and strongly supported. Fellow expatriates rallied contributions for the cost of the trip, which Adolphus could not afford, and arranged for her to stay with friends and relatives there.[15] At this time the dates for the National Championships and Wimbledon conflicted, and thus May's choice of Wimbledon compelled her to relinquish her American title. In England she entered local tournaments as preparation and returned to London in late June for Wimbledon's All-England Tournament. Once again she breezed through to the finals, which were then a challenge round pitting the recent victor against the winner from the previous year. Anticipating "a battle royal," hundreds of fans flocked to the courts believing Sutton's opponent to be a stalwart defender of English pride. Like Moore and Sutton at the National Championships, Dorothea Douglass had played Wimbledon as a teenager and won the tournament the past two years. She gave Sutton her first serious test and the close match everyone wanted. The first set was nip and tuck, though May eventually triumphed 6–3. In the second the players battled through five deuce games to a tense tie of 4–4. When Sutton finally pulled ahead 5–4, Douglass "gave way under the strain," and May ripped off four consecutive unchallenged points for game, set, and match. Her final ace elicited a crowd ovation that had "never been equaled on the English courts."[16]

Afterward Douglass graciously told the press, "May Sutton is a phenomenon."[17] However, Sutton had already surmised what leaked out afterward—Douglass was hampered by a badly sprained wrist and probably would have defaulted had the match not been so important. This injury fired Sutton's determination to return the following year and convince skeptics that she could conquer a healthy Douglass.

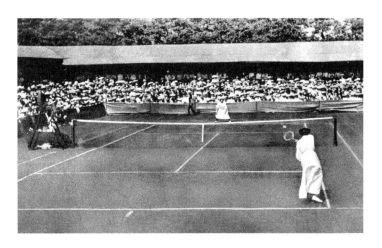

25. May Sutton versus Dorothea Douglass
(*foreground, right*), Wimbledon, 1905.
(Getty Images, Popperfoto Collection, 79038749)

The *New York Times* reported that during her first visit to England, May had not lost a single one of her 32 sets and only 75 of her 204 games, a winning percentage "not even approached by any of the women or men lawn tennis experts."[18]

The difficulty of sustaining such extraordinary success surfaced the following year at the North Counties Championships in Liverpool, where Sutton lost the finals of women's doubles. One observer auspiciously remarked that she "was especially weak at the net" and that "her strong point [was] not in doubles."[19] As the reigning champion at Wimbledon, Sutton was exempted from singles until the challenge round, but she was sorely taxed in doubles. In the third round she and her partner got into a thicket of tie games that extended to 12–10. The 6–4 second set was shorter, but no easier.[20] Her 10–8, 6–4 victory in the finals left Sutton depleted for singles against Douglass, who blasted her 6–1 in the first set.

Though she recovered in the second and gamely extended her opponent to 9–7, she lost, and her long string of undefeated sets and matches finally ended.

Instead of brooding over this dispiriting loss, Sutton immediately committed herself to proving that her first Wimbledon victory was no fluke. "I am not discouraged by my defeat, and I should like to have another go at it," she announced to the New York press and explained: "Miss Douglass played infinitely better than she did when I defeated her. There is no question but that I won the title when she was off-color, and that she was seriously handicapped by her accident, as was said at the time. This year she played superbly and was unapproachable, but I think as I improve my game there is a chance to beat her. I certainly mean to do it if it is possible for me."[21] Tell-tale indications that her confidence may have suffered more than she was admitting surfaced during a return stop in Newport, where she lost again in doubles, this time to a pair that included Mrs. Maud Barger-Wallach, a prominent, well-connected New Yorker who had reached the finals at the National Championships that year and won the tournament two years later.[22]

In April 1907 Sutton's plans for her rematch incurred a demoralizing setback when Douglass announced that she was marrying R. L. Chambers and would not play the All-England Tournament that summer.[23] By this point May had invested so much preparation and raised so many contributions that she was unwilling to change her plans. Moreover, Wimbledon was not her only objective. Her departure for England that month included a stop in New York for a tournament at the St. Nicholas Rink, where Mrs. Barger-Wallach was slated to play. Sutton and a local player reached the finals in doubles and thrashed Barger-Wallach and her partner 6–2, 6–2. "Aggressive and agile Miss May Sutton almost single handed carried off her match in the finals of women's lawn tennis doubles yesterday," one account reported. "The abounding physical vigor of Miss Sutton never slacked. She practically insisted in trying to cover the entire court on her side of the net. She was constantly on the run, and it was no unusual thing for her to hit the ball with her racquet when she was in the act of leaping toward it and with both feet off the ground."[24] A reader of this report might assume that Sutton was simply playing better than the year before, but another reporter detected a darker element in her 6–1, 6–1 decimation of Barger-Wallach in singles: "The scoring was one-sided, for almost invariably Miss Sutton shot the ball over the net when she had Mrs. Barger-Wallach at close range for a pass. By holding to these tactics Miss Sutton made a short match of the final, as her opponent made only feeble and futile attempts to check her."[25] Having established that her previous loss to Barger-Wallach was a miscue, Sutton sailed for England and Wimbledon. There she raced through the preliminary rounds and finals and was surprised to learn that Douglass had changed her mind and would defend her title in the challenge round. However, May easily dispatched her 6–1, 6–2. "At no part of yesterday's match," the *London Times* observed, "did the success of the American lady appear in doubt."[26]

Sutton's second Wimbledon title affirmed her to be the best player in women's tennis, but it also exhausted her meager financial support. A consortium of Los Angeles country clubs had rallied to cover the costs of her recent returns to Wimbledon.[27] But they had also advised her that future support would have to come from elsewhere. At this point the shorter, less expensive trip to the National Championships would have been a logical alternative, but May had so devastated Mrs. Barger-Wallach, its most promising contender, why bother? Why not, she reasoned, enjoy a relaxing summer and reconnect with her family? Perhaps some newcomer would emerge and inspire her to shoulder the ordeal of raising money and traveling across the country. As she looked east and scanned the horizon, little did she suspect that the opponent for whom she was searching would appear nearby.

Hazel Hotchkiss was a native Californian whose parents grew up along the Russian River and started their family in Healdsburg at a time when the area was better known for produce than grapes and wine. Born on December 20, 1886, three months after May, Hazel likewise came from a large family, hers consisting of four older brothers and another who was two years younger. As a frail, sickly child, she was a constant source of concern, but her early involvement in the activities of her brothers improved her health and encouraged her athleticism. Meanwhile, her father's failure with a prune business spurred him to try canning, which surged and quickly spawned sixteen plants around Northern California. When he became president of the Del Monte Corporation, he relocated its corporate headquarters to San Francisco and purchased a home for his family in Berkeley.[28]

Fourteen years old at the time of this move, Hazel had already achieved her fully developed, diminutive size of five feet and believed that she would likely be plain and ordinary.[29] "To get confidence in herself," she would later remark, "a girl who isn't attractive—or who thinks she isn't attractive—has

26. Hazel Hotchkiss, ca. 1908.
(From *American Lawn Tennis*, September 15, 1910, 290)

to do something well that other people admire."[30] Heeding her own advice, she took up tennis. In 1902, the year that May won her second Pacific States title, the University of California built an asphalt tennis court, and Hazel and her brothers began playing there. Since girls were not allowed on the court after 8:00 a.m., she had to roust her brothers at 5:00 to play with her. Like May's sisters, the Hotchkiss boys were intent on improving and were soon traveling to local tournaments with their younger sister. After only six months of play, Hazel entered a tournament in San Francisco and won women's doubles with a partner she met on the ferry to the city. In 1904 she scored her first major victory when she won singles at the nearby California State Championships.[31]

Sometime between his daughter's first tournament and her recent success, William Hotchkiss commissioned a concrete tennis court for his children.[32] As with May this new court contributed enormously to Hazel's improvement. The fact that her siblings were brothers rather than sisters profoundly influenced her style of play, and she would always emulate men players. At a tournament in San Rafael, she saw May play for the first time but came away more impressed by a doubles exhibition involving the Hardy brothers. As she later explained, "Doubles the way Sam and Sumner played—now *that* appealed to me. They were awfully quick at net play, and even a greenhorn like myself could appreciate the precision with which they volleyed and smashed, and their split-second maneuvers for drawing their opponent out of position and setting up their openings. I decided that afternoon that I'd go in for tennis and model my game on the Hardys'."[33] Unlike Sutton, whose intensity and athleticism appeared masculine, Hotchkiss emulated the strokes and movements of male players, especially the ones used in doubles.[34] She quickly progressed from a fourth in doubles with her brothers to mixed doubles involving top-flight male players—initially with the Sumner brothers and eventually with Maurice "Rocket" McLaughlin, who later won three National Championships in doubles. Hotchkiss invited McLaughlin and his friends to her court in order to learn their tactics. She quickly became as well known for her volleys, chops, and overheads as May was for her forehand. In contrast to Sutton, who annihilated genteel opponents with her unique forehand, Hotchkiss developed short-game shots that were more diverse and equally innovative. Although neither campaigned on behalf of their styles of play, they demonstrated them, and observers, especially ones in the East, noticed and judged them to be products of an environment that nurtured superior play. They were Californians and vanguards of a revolution mistakenly credited to better known successors—Helen Wills, Helen Jacobs, and Alice Marble. They successfully turned attention away from the proper, mannerly English game to the more diversified, more competitive one emerging on the West Coast. "The California girl," May would assert in a 1912 article, "is a better player than the girl from the East or Middle West for she can, if she desires, play the year round."[35] California's warmth, many tournaments, and hard court surfaces encouraged women players to develop speed and agility rather than gracefulness, strong tactics and athletic shots rather than social contacts.

In 1906, after winning singles at the California State Championships a second time, Hotchkiss entered the Pacific Coast Championships while May was away in England and beat Ethel, her first victory over one of the Sutton sisters.

In 1907, before starting her freshman year at the University of California, she reached the finals of the Pacific States Championships for the first time but lost a close match to Florence.[36] The July following her first year at Berkeley, she returned to the Pacific States Championships and again reached the finals, but lost this time to May by a respectable 6–3, 6–2.[37] That fall George Wright, who was touring with several accomplished players from the East, learned of Hazel's accomplishments and urged her parents to send her to the 1909 National Championships.[38]

William Hotchkiss was wealthy enough that funding for Hazel's tennis was never the problem it was for May. On the other hand, May's home in Southern California afforded her better playing conditions and a higher caliber of competition than Hazel had in the north. Thus when William agreed to underwrite Hazel's trip to the National Championships, he and his daughter agreed that she should prepare with as much winter play in Los Angeles as her academic schedule would allow. In February she reached the finals at the Coronado tournament and again faced Florence. This time Hazel prevailed 7–5, 9–7 in a stirring exhibition of long, exciting rallies and closely contested points, but she lost the challenge round to May, who had won every year since the tournament's inception in 1906. Although Sutton's easy victory made their much-anticipated match a disappointment, *American Lawn Tennis* reported that "Miss Hotchkiss took more games from Miss Sutton than any of the local experts [were] able to," winning two in the first and three in the second set.[39] Hazel next won the Ojai Valley tournament, which the Suttons did not attend because they had been invited to visit Mexico.

At the National Championships, Hotchkiss swept through the first four rounds without losing a set. However, she was hard pressed in the finals against Louise Hammond. Thus far Hotchkiss had enjoyed enormous success by taking the net and volleying, but Hammond's passing shots were so successful that Hazel retreated to the baseline and tried long rallies, but she still lost the first set 6–8. When Hammond appeared to weary in the second set, Hazel resumed her attack and overwhelmed her opponent 6–1 with a withering barrage of overheads. Hotchkiss sustained her momentum to a 3–1 lead in the final set, but instead of breaking Hammond battled back to 4–5. Behind 0–40 in the next game, Louise clawed her way back to 30–40 before a final double fault cost her the match.[40]

In the challenge round Hotchkiss faced Mrs. Barger-Wallach, the winner from the previous year. Though Barger-Wallach had an imposing record and reputation, Hotchkiss quickly found her to be a lame opponent. Now in her late thirties, she had been in such poor health prior to the tournament that she nearly withdrew. Against Hazel she was practically inept; she had no backhand, moved poorly, avoided the net, and lost by the lopsided score of 1–6, 0–6. Hotchkiss later commented, "How she had ever won the singles I'll never know."[41] Although this defeat was worse than Sutton's rout of Barger-Wallach three years before, Hotchkiss played the second set so that it appeared to be more of a contest, feeding Barger-Wallach's forehand and creating long rallies — a decision that won her additional points. Unlike May, Hazel had deep respect for the politeness and sportsmanship of the traditional game. A veteran United States Lawn Tennis Association (USLTA) official who witnessed and vividly remembered this match observed decades later, "I don't think Hazel's courtesy toward Mrs. Barger-Wallach was lost on many of us who saw her on that first trip East."[42]

Hotchkiss saved her A-game for doubles and mixed doubles and won both of them as well. A *New York Times* account of her triple victory observed: "The consensus of critical opinion is that Miss Hotchkiss is the greatest woman player ever seen here, with the possible exception of Miss [May] Sutton. With a powerful backhand and forehand drive she is a lightning volleyer, and in overhead play is stronger than Miss Sutton."[43]

May noticed Hazel's improvement before the National Championships validated it, but she had beaten her so easily in their previous meetings that she still did not consider her a serious threat. Early in 1909, before Hazel announced her intent to play at the National Championships, May informed reporters that she would compete there.[44] However, unforeseen developments derailed these plans. For months May and her parents had been wondering how much longer she was going to allow tennis to dominate her life. Should she not be thinking more about her future and finding a livelihood? Earlier she had applied to be a girls' basketball coach at the Troop School in Pasadena, but this position necessitated that she also be a teacher, and May had never been good student and did not attend college.[45] She realized that she lacked the temperament and patience to teach tennis and knew all too well that the pay was poor and uncertain. Such thinking almost certainly factored into an early July announcement that she was engaged to Harry B. Hall, a banker in Mexico City, and would not be going to Philadelphia.[46] A month later May concluded that Hall was not husband material and broke her engagement. In an aside to this announcement, she quipped that women ought not to marry until they were over twenty-five and provoked a torrid debate that persisted for months.[47]

Sutton's romance kept her away from tennis for six months, but Hotchkiss's triumphs in the East stoked May's determination to reaffirm her superiority.[48] The California State Championships was a tournament that Hotchkiss had won the past three years. The Hotel Rafael, which hosted this event, was located north of San Francisco and so far away that the Suttons rarely participated. Learning that Hazel was scheduled to play again, the sisters agreed to play too. Unfortunately, the ladder routed Florence to meet May, who again eliminated her.

American Lawn Tennis reported that the challenge round between May and Hazel attracted "the greatest crowd in the history of the game in California." The first set was a tense battle of contrasts — Hazel cutting to the net at every opportunity and May hugging the baseline and drilling passing shots. At 2–2, Sutton broke Hotchkiss's serve, but Hazel came back in the next game and evened the score to 4–4. May prevailed in the next two games and took the first set. With bolstered confidence she swiftly took command of the second set and won 6–1.[49]

At the Coronado tournament the following spring, Hotchkiss again prevailed over Florence 3–6, 6–1, 6–1. May successfully avenged her sister's defeat, but the final score was a much closer 6–3, 3–6, 6–4. The second set was the first one that Hazel took from May. Although she lost the deciding set, she established that the gap between her and May had narrowed. Grim and resolute, Sutton bolted to a

27. Hazel Hotchkiss at the 1909 National Championships.

(From *American Lawn Tennis*, July 1, 1909, 82)

three-game lead in the final set. After Hazel won her serve, May took hers and claimed a commanding 4–1 lead. Instead of crumbling Hotchkiss bore down and won the next three games to even the score. Sutton's relentless drives secured her the final two games, and they proved to be the margin of difference in the total games each won.[50]

A 6–2, 6–3 thrashing of Hotchkiss at a tournament in Long Beach a week later reassured May of her unassailable superiority.[51] At Ojai, an event she had dominated for years but conceded to Hazel while she was in Mexico, May learned that her close match at Coronado was no fluke and suffered her first loss. The seemingly close, three-set score of 6–2, 4–6, 0–6 revealed, to close scrutiny, that when challenged, Sutton was vulnerable to disintegration.[52] Sutton was so shaken by her third-set collapse that she spurned the traditional handshake and tromped off the court without speaking to Hotchkiss.

This devastating loss convinced Sutton that Hotchkiss had developed into a potent, dangerous adversary. The surging popularity of their epic battles also created a golden opportunity for organizers, and they moved quickly to arrange an exhibition between the champions over the Memorial Day weekend at a palatial, recently opened resort in the mountains east of Los Angeles. The 3,000 spectators who flocked to this event vastly exceeded the seating for 1,500, which already far surpassed normal attendance for the finals of the National Championships.[53] Many had to park their cars far down the hill and accept seating on rooftops. Whether or not May calculated the sums of money being harvested, she certainly registered them. Off the court she was helpless against tennis's entrenched and uncompromising code of amateurism. Since its inception and for many years more, the game's dominant players would come from wealth and tap it in order to compete. Even though May herself was from a family with its own tennis court, financing for her trips had long been a source of frustration and frequently soured her attitude toward more-privileged opponents—notably Barger-Wallach and Hazel. May, of course, received some remuneration, but it would have helped little with her problematic lack of livelihood. Like Billy Jean King later, she must have resented the money going into the pockets of others from exploitation of her celebrity.

May also realized that she had to stifle her resentment, be alert to the threat Hazel posed, and concentrate on this match. Her tense 6–3, 4–6, 6–2 reversal of the scores at Ojai was a gratifying vindication and so thrilling that the *Los Angeles Times* awarded the event featured, multipage coverage and numerous photographs.[54]

Again May elected not to challenge Hotchkiss at the upcoming National Championships. The familiar problem of funding would have influenced this decision, but May's rationale was more deeply rooted in a legitimate belief that both of them stood head and shoulders above the competition, and despite the closeness of their recent matches, Hazel had only beaten her a single time. Would a title in Philadelphia prove anything that she had not already accomplished in California?[55]

This decision freed Hotchkiss to contend with Mrs. Barger-Wallach and Louise Hammond, and neither of them performed any better than they had the year before. Hotchkiss successfully defended all three of her titles, and *American Lawn Tennis* offered this summary of her achievement:

"Thus the battle was waged again, and this time there remains no doubt of the California girl's superiority. She won in straight sets and at no time did there appear to be much doubt as to the result."[56]

Prior to her visit to Philadelphia, Hotchkiss agreed to return to California via Los Angeles and play a Long Beach exhibition match against May Sutton. Hazel accepted this invitation without adequately anticipating the adverse effects of her week of hard tennis in Philadelphia and the grueling cross-country train ride back. With scant down time between her arrival in Los Angeles and this event, she was flat for her match, and May offered no mercy in her 6–2, 6–0 thrashing. "In fact," one observer commented, "the match seemed a reversion to those days when Miss Sutton stood head and shoulders above any possible rival in this territory, and one almost wondered if, after all, the present national champion was not battling against someone completely above her class."[57]

This time Hotchkiss felt bushwhacked. Convinced that she had played below her potential, she fastened on the Pacific States Championships in September as an opportunity for redemption. At this point in her career, Hotchkiss's reaction to defeat differed markedly from Sutton's. Since she lost more frequently and was never the dominant player May was, she did not allow the loss of a game, a set, or even a match to upset her. Unlike Sutton, who brooded and grew more intense when she played poorly, Hotchkiss responded to setbacks and mistakes as though they were learning opportunities; she experimented with her shots and rhythm, calmly jettisoning what did not work and constantly searching for chinks in her opponent. Because Sutton's strength was her forehand, Hotchkiss practiced hard to develop a repertoire of shots for her backhand. "There are some veteran tennis fans," Herbert Wind once observed, "who think that [Hazel's] years of furious concentration on breaking down May Sutton's backhand left such an indelible mark on her that she has automatically played everyone's backhand ever since."[58]

Although May had skipped the Pacific States Championships the year before, Hazel was confident she would be at the upcoming one at the elegant Del Monte Hotel on the already famous seventeen-mile drive of the Monterey Peninsula. During preliminary rounds both she and Sutton were challenged in opening sets, but both overwhelmed their opponents in the second and won handily. "The final match between Miss Hotchkiss and Miss May Sutton," *American Lawn Tennis* reported, "evoked more enthusiasm than any tennis ever before seen at Del Monte and the players responded by furnishing one of the most sensational matches in coast tennis history."[59] As usual Sutton started strong and surged to a three-game lead. Hotchkiss retained her cool and snatched two games, but lost the two that followed, which gave Sutton a 5–2 lead. Hazel tenaciously battled back to even the score. In an all-too-familiar finish, May surged to take the two games necessary for the set. With a come-back flourish of inspired tennis, Hotchkiss raced out to a 5–1 lead in the second set. This time Sutton refused to buckle. Willfully suppressing her bitter memory of the disastrous third set at Ojai, she salvaged three straight games. But Hotchkiss ended her run with a win that awarded her the second set. The final set was a war of nerves and even scores—2–2, 3–3, 4–4. The final two games involved prolonged exchanges and several deuces, but again Sutton took the late games that decided the match.[60]

Years later Hotchkiss would claim that Sutton's bold but unsuccessful surge at the end of the second set had left her spent and vulnerable. In order to regroup and cool her opponent, May insisted on a prolonged tea break.[61] This gamesmanship tactic transformed their contentious rivalry into a bitter hostility. During future warm-ups, Sutton would either withhold the ball or intentionally hit it well outside the lines.[62] In an uncharacteristic display of ill will years later, Hotchkiss admitted to an interviewer, "She [Sutton] was very hard for me to play against because she was not ladylike—she was rude, she was unsportsmanlike—and it upset me."[63] Sutton did not merely defeat Hotchkiss; she rattled her emotional control, and Hazel vowed not to let that happen again.

The following spring Hotchkiss did not play Coronado, Ojai, or the Southern California Championships, but she did agree to participate in a midwinter tournament in Long Beach. Demanding school work constrained her time for practice, and May exploited her rustiness with a convincing 7–5, 6–1 victory.[64] This match reaffirmed May's superiority over Hotchkiss and caused her to reflect on how her recent string of victories had had the unfortunate effect of marginalizing and demoralizing Florence. During their meeting at the recent Pacific States Championships, she crushed her sister 6–1, 6–2 and routed her by similar scores in two subsequent meetings.[65] Nonetheless, Florence was playing as well as ever and consistently beating everyone else; she had even beaten Hazel the year before in straight sets. But whenever Florence ran into May, she was doomed. Given the strength of her play recently and her age of twenty-eight, Florence knew she would not remain a top-flight player for much longer. What if, the sisters speculated, Florence went to Philadelphia and May stayed home? Wasn't Florence likely to meet Hotchkiss in either the semifinals or the finals? When the two sisters learned that, as a graduation present, William was funding Hazel to participate for a third time and to play several satellite tournaments as well, they agreed that Florence should enter the same events. If Florence were to win several of these events, she could break away from May's shadow and claim the spotlight Hazel enjoyed.

However, this plan faltered from the outset when Florence lost preliminary tournaments in Philadelphia and Pittsburgh.[66] These losses did not upset her because she was accustomed to California hard courts and was playing these events as preparation for the grass courts at the Philadelphia Cricket Club. When the National Championships started a week later, she vindicated this decision by mowing down her early opponents. For the challenge round against Hotchkiss, she was understandably nervous, and her tentativeness allowed Hazel to open up a 4–1 lead. But she settled down and worked her way back to 4–4. The ensuing games went back and forth to 8–8, when Florence, like May, pushed ahead to claim the set. Although Florence's surge continued through the first game of the next set, Hotchkiss steadied, ran off six consecutive games, and took the second set. Through five of these games, Hazel lost only eight points. At this point Florence repeated May's ploy at Del Monte and took a seven-minute break. Although her play improved following this break, so did Hazel's and she soon had a 4–3 lead. Florence countered and won back the lead 5–4. When she failed to

28. Hazel Hotchkiss, 1910.
(Library of Congress, LC-USZ62-93999)

take the critical next game, the match settled into another deadlock that extended to 7–7. Finally, Hazel volleyed her way to victory.[67]

This razor-thin defeat devastated Florence. Two weeks later at another tournament in Pittsburgh, she lost to Hotchkiss by a lopsided score of 1–6, 2–6. When their paths crossed again at the Metropolitan Championships in New York City, Hazel blasted her 6–1, 6–1.[68]

By Florence's third loss, May had already departed from

California and reached Buffalo so that she was there when
Florence arrived. For several days they practiced together
in preparation for the Niagara event. Luckily, Florence was
bracketed so that she would meet Hazel before May. When
they faced each other in the third round, Florence quickly
demonstrated that May's support and advice had rescued her
from the nosedive of the past month. Playing with a grit and
focus not seen since the Championships, she kept the first set
even until 5–5 and then snatched the next two games and
the set. But again her momentum gave out, and she lost the
second set 0–6. As in Philadelphia she managed a game third
set, but Hotchkiss prevailed 6–4.[69]

Over the two years between Hotchkiss's first title at the
National Championships and the impending final at Niagara, she and May had played each other nine times. Sutton
won eight of these matches—six were convincing victories;
two were close, three-set wins; and the ninth was Hotchkiss's lone triumph at Ojai.[70] All these encounters had been
on either asphalt or dirt, and Niagara would be their first
meeting on grass. As they took the court, which of their previous matches did each recall? Was it one she had won? Or
one she lost? Perhaps it was one that extended and tested her,
or one she had played especially well, or one that exposed a
weakness to be exploited. Most likely they ignored the past
and concentrated on the contest at hand.

May had always started strong, and she did so once
again, like a rocket. She took all of the first six games, losing only eight points. Hotchkiss had fallen behind repeatedly in the early going of previous matches, but this set
finished before she could adjust or win a single game. She
was stunned—nothing she tried was even able to extend the

games. Even worse, Sutton continued her blitzkrieg through the first three games of the second set. Finally Hotchkiss won a game, but Sutton resumed her march through the next two.

At this point Sutton had won eleven of their twelve games and needed only one more to claim the match and annihilate the reigning National Champion. At least Hazel had the serve—and a helpful bit of advice. A linesman pointed out that a soft drizzle had dampened the court and suggested that the players replace their shoes with ones that had allowable spikes. Sutton was so pleased with how everything was going that she elected not to change. Dazed though she was, Hotchkiss donned her spikes and mentally prepared for a heavier ball. This amended course of action at this critical juncture furnished Hazel what she needed most: hope and a strategy. She was also aided by her experience of climbing out of deep holes against Sutton twice before. When play resumed, Hazel pressured May's unsure footing, keeping the ball in play and making her run.[71] And it worked. First she won her serve at 40–15. In the next game she got the point she needed to push the 30–40 score to love and proceeded to snatch the game. The momentum was reversed. As Sutton grew tentative and anxious, Hotchkiss attacked more vigorously and claimed the three games that gave her the set.[72]

Up to this point Sutton had lost very few sets and never one in which she held such a commanding lead. Having failed to capture a single one of the four games that would have given her the match, she lost not only the second set but all six games of the final set, thirteen consecutive games.

What had nearly been Sutton's greatest margin of victory over Hotchkiss suddenly disintegrated into a nightmare defeat, her worst by far. Stealing herself against the pain, she fastened on upcoming events in Buffalo and Pittsburgh, which Hotchkiss was scheduled to play. However, Hazel skipped Buffalo and announced that an injured foot prevented her from playing Pittsburgh.[73] She opted instead for a tournament in Boston at the Longwood Cricket Club. With no Suttons and weak competition, she relaxed, won easily, and finished her four-month tour undefeated. At social events there she met and fell in love with George William Wightman, a recent graduate of Harvard and a member of its tennis team.[74] Three months later, on February 24, 1912, they married and settled into a house on the Wightman estate near the Longwood Cricket Club, where she would later train several prominent champions.

Meanwhile, Tom Bundy consoled May. A group photograph from the Niagara tournament shows Bundy seated at the end of the first row, but he did not compete there.[75] He was included in the picture because he was a well-known player and happened to be there. Currently ranked no. 2 in singles, he and Maurice McLaughlin had recently teamed up to play doubles, and they would later win the National Championships in 1912, 1913, and 1914. As veterans of many tournaments in Southern California, Sutton and Bundy had known each other for years, but their presence at the Niagara event bespoke a deepening relationship. Both participated in the Buffalo tournament and played as partners at an exhibition of mixed doubles in Syracuse several days later.[76] The following year, on December 11, 1912, they were married in Los Angeles and settled into a new home in Brentwood.[77]

Thus situated at opposite ends of the country, May and

Hazel immediately started families, and over the decade that followed, May had four children and Hazel had five. Had they opted instead to play each year at the National Championships or Wimbledon, there would have been many more memorable matches, and one of them might have emerged the greatest champion ever. But at the time both chose families instead, never imagining that these exclusive, small-crowd tournaments would become the premiere events they are today.

Nonetheless, both also believed that motherhood and tennis need not be an exclusive choice.[78] They continued to compete intermittently, and their successes were extraordinary. Mary K. Browne won the National Championships in 1912, 1913, and 1914, but during the trip that produced her second title, she played Hazel and lost. Hazel returned to the National Championships in 1915, following the birth of her second child, and lost the finals to Molla Bjurstedt, whose record of eight singles titles there has never been bested. Following the birth of her third child, Hazel retuned to the National Championships in 1919 and overwhelmed Marion Zinderstein in the finals of singles.

The same year that Hazel lost to Molla Bjurstedt in the finals of the National Championships, May, who had two children, played Molla at a special Thanksgiving match in Long Beach and beat her.[79] A month later she won a second exhibition against her.[80] Two years later, when her third child was a year old, May prevailed a third time.[81] In 1921 she mounted a comeback and achieved a no. 3 position in that year's ranking, but lost to Mary K. Browne in the semifinals of the National Championships.[82]

During a 1920 return to California, Hazel met and

befriended the fifteen-year-old Helen Wills. Believing the young player to be an exceptional talent, she extended her stay to coach Wills and afterward invited her to Boston for additional mentoring. In 1922 Wills defeated May in the semifinals at Forest Hills, though she did not win her first title until a year later.[83] In 1924 Hazel teamed up with Wills to play doubles, and the pair won the National Championships, the Olympics in Paris, and Wimbledon (Hazel's first victory there). They were never defeated.

This selective accounting of victories following their marriages affirms the remarkable durability of these two champions. Their paths did not cross over these years, but fate ordained them a final meeting at the USLTA Championships in Forest Hills, New York, in 1928. That year both decided to try singles for a last time and successfully battled their way into a third-round meeting. Odds makers favored May, who had several major victories to her credit, including one over Charlotte Hosmer Chapin, then ranked no. 3.

Twenty years before when the two women first played each other, May was the established champion and Hazel was an upstart from the North. Only a sprinkling of spectators showed up to watch this match, but two years later Hotchkiss was herself a National Champion and crowds flocked to watch their matches. Both were not only the best women players in California but indisputably the best in the game. The skill and intensity of their play were major factors in the surging popularity of tennis and its transformation from recreation for genteel ladies into strenuous competition. Not until both married and scaled back on their involvement did tennis develop a pool of players with as much ability.

This 1928 match of former titlists in Forest Hills did not fill the three-year-old horseshoe stadium that accommodated thirteen thousand, but it was constructed as a stage for Helen Wills after her 1923 triumph at the National Championships returned the title to an American for the first time in four years.[84] Those who accepted "Little Miss Poker Face" as an apt characterization of Wills's personality and style of play did not realize how much this nickname owed to Hazel's training and her accumulated experience against May.

As the two women, at the remarkable ages of forty-two, took the court and surveyed the grandeur of their setting, they realized that the game had grown far bigger than they ever imagined, but their advancement to this round also reassured them that they remained among its top players. And their final encounter was another close one. Hazel nipped May 6–4 in first set. Fittingly, the second set was tense and extended, but Hazel prevailed 11–9.[85]

In 1940 Hazel and May divorced their husbands, moved on to senior events, and racked up more victories. Their lives intersected a final time at the end. Hazel was eighty-seven when she died on December 5, 1974. Less than a year later, on October 4, 1975, May succumbed at the age of eighty-eight.

FIVE

Barney Oldfield

People's Champion and Threat to Early Automobile Racing

The contest featured classic ingredients—an aging celebrity champion against a younger star in his prime with a backdrop of bad blood between them. In this case the sport was insistently modern: automobile racing. Barney Oldfield and Ralph De Palma had agreed to compete against each other in the 1914 Vanderbilt Cup, which was to be held for the first time in California. Oldfield's victories over the previous twelve years made him America's best-known driver. He had witnessed the advent of the horseless carriage and capitalized on it to achieve fame and fortune. A reunion with friends from his bicycle-racing past introduced him to auto racing, produced a momentous victory at Grosse Pointe in 1902, and led to a well-planned series of two-car matches and speed exhibitions. Continuing success ratcheted up his percentage of gate receipts and embellished his reputation as the speed demon who first cracked the mile-a-minute barrier. Needing an improved vehicle in order to sustain his momentum, he opted for a lucrative contract to drive for an automobile maker and became America's first professional driver. Eventually he abandoned this sponsorship and assembled a collection of cars and drivers that enabled him to dictate appearance fees, avoid collisions, and orchestrate dramatic finishes. As he took the track, he would shout to the crowd, "You know me, Barney Oldfield!" and it would bellow back that it did indeed know him. The unlit cigar originally used to protect his clinched teeth was interpreted by fans as evidence of his fearlessness and quickly became his trademark.

Thus pitted against the king of speed and the master of hype, De Palma, like *anyone* opposing Oldfield, faced a formidable challenge. A sudden need for a replacement vaulted him to a driving position with Fiat, currently the dominant team in racing. As he developed into its best driver, he cultivated an identity radically different from Oldfield's. He was the loyal, self-effacing member of an organization—a team player who respected others, the rules, and the cause of serious racing.

Nonetheless, it was the Contest Board of the American Automobile Association (AAA) that infused this rivalry with special significance. The board's early efforts to regulate the rampant profusion of races and to check Oldfield's headstrong independence were hampered by inadequate authority. However, the development of new "purpose-built" racers by European manufacturers created fresh opportunities for premiere, multicar events and for the Contest Board to supervise them. Convinced that he remained above the Contest Board and its regulations, Oldfield persisted with his reckless course until a disastrous confrontation forced him out of racing. His return necessitated that he accept the board's authority, relinquish his privileged status, and for the first time in years, drive cars others owned. This final need intensified his feud with De Palma and made their antagonistic encounter at the Vanderbilt race in Santa Monica one of the greatest races ever.

Barney Oldfield was born in a log cabin in Wauseon, Ohio, and was fourteen when his father quit his hardscrabble farm and relocated his family to Toledo. Within a year Barney had dropped out of school and started a series of menial jobs. The surging popularity of the new safety bicycle, which started the Workmans on their ambitious trips, inspired him to acquire one and to compete in local races. In 1895 he finished second in three events at the Ohio State Championships and parlayed this success into a paid position with the Stearns Bicycle Company. The enormous popularity of racing the new bicycles and strong backing from prosperous manufacturers pressured the League of American Wheelmen to drop its long-standing opposition to professionalism, and soon it was even endorsing purse events. August Zimmerman and Eddie Bald became so famous for their racing prowess during the 1890s that they were able to command special appearance fees and endorsements that rocketed their incomes beyond those of the highest-paid baseball players.[1]

Although Oldfield competed against top racers, he never made the big money his friend and fellow racer Tom Cooper did. By the late 1890s crowds flocked to watch Cooper challenge Bald, and he won the prestigious Bicycle Championships of America in 1899. The *New York Times* once described Cooper as "arguably the richest racing cyclist in the world today," but a crop of new talent abruptly curtailed his success.[2] Devastating losses to Major Taylor and Frank Kramer spurred him to quit racing at the end of the 1900 season.[3]

After a foray into mining out West, Cooper decided that his cycling experience and nest egg could be put to better use in auto racing and looked up Henry Ford, whom he had met and advised at a racing triumph of the young automaker over Alexander Winton. Ford's impressive showing of his recently completed vehicle against this successful manufacturer secured him financing for commercial production, but his backers were so intent on attracting customers and so opposed to racing that he soon regretted their contractual agreement. Thus during their reconnection in the spring of 1902, Cooper found Ford discontented and pining for a return to racing. When Cooper agreed to finance construction of a new race car, Ford promptly sold out his interest in the Henry Ford Company, but his retention of rights to his name necessitated that the company be renamed Cadillac.[4]

Ford launched construction on two racing cars that were identical except for slight differences in their exhaust systems. As with the Model T, which later won him success and fame, Ford made simplicity his guiding principle. "The machine is chiefly remarkable," announced an early report, "for the extent to which it has been stripped of all unnecessary or superfluous weight."[5] It had no body, no springs on the rear axle, no differential, only a single forward gear, and a rude brake. Cooper's bicycle experience undoubtedly influenced the vehicle's unusual handlebar steering, which replaced a problem-plagued steering wheel on Ford's original racer. The white ash, steel-plated chassis had both the widest wheelbase and the largest motor of any racer to date. The seventy-horsepower engine, roughly three times more powerful than the one in his first machine, was situated behind an imposing ribbed radiator and required a driver with strength, daring, and instantaneous judgment.[6] "The roar of those cylinders alone was enough to half kill a man," Ford observed. "We let them out at full speed. I cannot quite describe the sensation. Going over Niagara Falls would have been but a pastime after a ride in one of them."[7]

Why Ford elected to build two versions of the same machine is not clear. It is possible that his agreement with Cooper stipulated a car for each of them. Perhaps they were also thinking that one would turn out better than the other. Whatever the rationale Ford lost confidence in the project as the cars neared completion. Early on he knew that he did not want to drive his monsters. "I did not want to take the responsibility of racing," Ford acknowledged, "and neither did Cooper."[8] Cooper, of course, was the experienced racer and therefore expected to drive. However, Ford's wife, Clara, disliked Cooper and her husband's involvement with racing. Ford himself already knew that his best hope for success lay with a commercial product and that he should concentrate on it. He also had grave reservations about the two automobiles, which were hard to start and even harder to keep running. Thus, before either one had actually raced, Ford sold both cars to Cooper.[9]

Unlike Ford, Cooper sensed an advantage in the two machines that he did not fully comprehend until months later: two machines furnished him the basic ingredients for a race. Cooper knew from his bicycle experience that crowds loved a promising duel and sensed that his two imposing machines could provide one. At this delicate moment when he was splitting with Ford, Cooper summoned Oldfield to join him in Detroit. While Cooper may have been seeking his friend's support with the unfolding stress and uncertainty, he needed another brave driver even more. Cooper's letter of invitation shrewdly flattered Barney for having "already earned

30. Barney Oldfield (*left*) and Tom Cooper, 1903.
(Oldfield Collection, LA84 Foundation)

a reputation for taking chances."[10] Like Ford, Cooper was apprehensive about the skittish, unwieldy cars, but he was prepared to handle one of them and was almost certainly thinking of Oldfield as a prospective driver for the other.

Shortly after Oldfield's arrival, Cooper took both cars to a race in Dayton, Ohio. This competition was arranged by Carl Fisher, a long-standing friend from professional bicycle racing and exceptional promoter who later developed both the Indianapolis 500 and Miami Beach. Fisher started with a bicycle shop in Indianapolis and an exclusive franchise from Colonel Pope to sell Columbia Standards. When he noticed the attention automobiles were attracting, he sensed opportunity and drew on his friendships with Ransom Olds and Winton to exploit it.[11] Olds's plant was annually manufacturing five thousand vehicles, a full quarter of total production; Winton, the second largest company, made only a thousand.[12] Fisher understood that people's curiosity about these strange machines greatly exceeded their willingness to purchase them. Believing that races would make these oddities exciting and desirable, he convinced Olds and Winton to furnish him vehicles as promotion.

The event in Dayton, the first of a slate Fisher was preparing, was devised as a sequence of pairings. The first race was between Oldsmobiles, and he and Earl Kiser, another bicycling buddy, competed against each other in Wintons. Fisher recruited Cooper to enter his two cars. Ford was undoubtedly pleased to learn that on the day of the races neither of his former cars was able to perform and their event had to be canceled. However, immediately following the final competition, Cooper suddenly streaked onto the track in one of the Fords and dashed off a fast lap. Fisher hurriedly arranged a timed mile, but Cooper's car again failed shortly after the start.[13]

An ensuing race at Grosse Pointe validated Cooper's risky investment and launched Oldfield's career. The program for this race listed Cooper as driver for the Manufacturers' Challenge Cup, which Ford had won the year before. Since two Wintons were participating in the same race, Cooper probably could have entered both Fords, but persisting mechanical problems left him with only one functional machine. Moreover, had the event not already been twice postponed, that car would not have been ready. The day of the race Cooper tapped Oldfield to drive his lone entry. Accounts afterward reported that Oldfield had driven for the first time only two days before.[14] Since Cooper had consistently outperformed Oldfield on bicycles and was much better known, this substitution would have been a difficult decision, and it is unlikely that he ever would have made it if these colorful reports had been accurate. Oldfield himself later admitted that he drove multiple times over the week before the race and probably had done so several times prior to that.[15] In other words, Cooper appointed Oldfield to drive his only available automobile because he undoubtedly had compelling evidence that Barney was a superior driver.

Unsure of both his ability and his machine, Oldfield relied on tactics from his bicycle experience to avoid difficult passes and go faster. Prior to the moving start, he dropped behind the other vehicles, increased his speed as the starting line approached, and bolted for the lead. Initially this plan produced a false start, but his second try succeeded, and he was never passed or seriously challenged. Observers were dazzled by the innovative way in which Barney whipped through curves and powered into the straightaways. Oldfield later described how he abandoned the conventional automobile practice of slowing for curves and opted to speed up for them instead. As he had routinely done on curves in bicycling, he controlled the eye-popping slide of his rear wheels with a deft angling of his front wheels against the spin.[16] *Motor Age* proclaimed him "a man absolutely devoid of realization of danger."[17] His car finished a full lap ahead of the second-place vehicle and set course records for a single lap and the five-mile distance. Since the fastest time for the mile had been lowered several times recently, spectators left believing that Oldfield's fleet car might be the first to crack the formidable mile-a-minute

31. Barney Oldfield at Columbus, 1903.
(Benson Ford Research Center, The Henry Ford)

barrier. In his promotion for the Dayton race, Fisher had dubbed the car "999," after the famous New York Central Railroad engine that first covered a mile under a minute.[18] Newspaper reports of the Grosse Pointe race registered the aptness of this name, and ensuing publicity exploited it.[19]

If Oldfield drew upon his bicycling experience to achieve this first victory, Cooper used his to exploit it. After splitting the $300 purse for winning at Grosse Pointe, he secured another $250 for allowing C and J Tires to advertise their endorsement.[20] Next, he negotiated a 25 percent cut of the proceeds for agreeing to participate in a Fisher event in Toledo the following weekend.[21] This time both machines operated, and Barney nipped Cooper in a thrilling contest. "The machines emit fire and water, and when they go past one instinctively feels that they are devils incarnate," reported one observer. "It was truly a great exhibition and would stir the blood of the most frigid individual in the country."[22]

Eager to stage more events before snow closed everything, Cooper contracted Grosse Pointe to host a series of post-Thanksgiving assaults by Oldfield on existing speed records. In return for switching tires, the Diamond Rubber Company agreed to post a $250 reward for each new record, and Barney bagged two.[23] "[His] mile record," trumpeted a Diamond postrace advertisement "is 1.3 seconds and [the] five mile record is 8 seconds under previous world's records."[24]

Over the winter Oldfield worked at an automotive shop in Toledo while Cooper improved both cars, especially the weaker Arrow, which was equipped with an overhead cam and repainted red. Glenn Stuart, an agent, was hired to book events with larger crowds, better press coverage, and higher stakes. When Stuart learned that Alexander Winton and Henri Fournier, the dominant racers during the previous season, were negotiating to race each other, he proposed a series of events that would include Oldfield and pay out fifty thousand dollars in purses.[25] Although this overblown scheme quickly deflated, Stuart's discussions with Alfred Reeves, manager of the Empire City Race Track outside New York City, generated a promising alternative. Like Grosse Pointe this track was originally built for horses but allowed cars to use the facility in order to alleviate financial strains and compensate for diminishing interest in this kind of racing. Reeves and Stuart persuaded Charles Wridgway, manager of the largest car dealerships in the New York area, to drive one of his new cars against Oldfield over the Memorial Day weekend.[26] Wridgway wanted the publicity, but Reeves had to guarantee Cooper and Oldfield 25 percent of the receipts, a fee that henceforth became their expectation.[27]

In the refurbished Arrow, renamed Red Devil, Oldfield

drove the first heat of the five-mile event only fast enough to win, nearly two minutes slower than his previous times for the distance. In the second heat he shot away at the start and finished almost two miles ahead. His second lap matched his December time, which was officially recognized this time as a world record.[28]

Carl Fisher was so impressed by the attendance and victory at Empire City that he contracted Oldfield and Cooper to race each other in the featured event of an Indianapolis program. He sweetened their appearance fee with a $250 award if either completed a mile under a minute.[29] Sensing that this event could burnish Oldfield's reputation and bolster returns from future events, Cooper kept Barney in the faster Red Devil, accepted the old 999, and did his best to stay in the race. Oldfield rewarded Fisher with a time of 59.6 seconds for one of his laps.[30] Although several other drivers had already completed a straightaway mile under a minute, Oldfield was the first to do so on a circular track. Afterward, billing for Oldfield routinely hyped him as *the* mile-a-minute man.

New York newspapers, which usually ignored events in the heartland, dutifully noted Oldfield's dazzling successes and furnished the resourceful manager of the Empire City track with a windfall opportunity to replace a canceled race between Fournier and Winton with one featuring Oldfield for "a Silver Trophy emblematic of the Track Championship of America."[31] After Barney won and lowered the mile record, the venerable *Scientific American*, influenced perhaps by earlier promotion of 999, reported that the "Ford-Cooper racer" (the upgraded Red Devil) went "faster than most express trains" and added:

Every time Oldfield's racer started to make a turn, even though he kept close to the outside fence and turned the front wheels very gradually, the rear end of the machine would skid around so far that the whole car appeared for the moment to be aiming straight for the inner fence. In an instant it would straighten out again, however, skim round the bend, and dart along the farther side of the course at more than express train speed, only to be seen a few seconds later making its last turn amid a cloud of dust, and then making its final rush down the home stretch.[32]

Motor Age viewed the race as proof that American cars were no longer inferior to those from Europe. "And yet Europeans say Americans cannot build racers," it snorted: "Rot! Just wait until our own dare-devil Barney gets the chance he is seeking for a straightaway mile."[33]

Afterward Alexander Winton signed Oldfield to a contract that paid him an annual fee of $2,500, covered the cost of mechanics and transportation, and allowed him to keep both his prize money and appearance fees.[34] At the time Oldfield and Cooper realized that their improvements had exhausted the potential of their two cars. In order to stay abreast of the competition they would either have to build or buy a new car, and the associated costs and risks were simply too great. Winton, on the other hand, had already compiled a formidable record of success and was currently finishing a new racer. His offer for Barney to pilot his Bullet no. 2 was impossible to beat. The carmaker also approved Oldfield's wish to adjust to his Winton with races against Cooper in the Red Devil.

By the time Oldfield reached Denver, he no longer needed an accommodating opponent and achieved new world records for the five-, ten-, and fifteen-mile distances.[35] Out in California he admitted to reporters that he "could tell, when driving the Bullet at its greatest speed, within one second of the time in which [he made] each mile."[36] Already he was deploying that knowledge to please crowds with new, split-second records.

During the early spring of 1904, Oldfield achieved a momentous victory over William K. Vanderbilt, *the* premiere example of the wealthy enthusiast who dominated early car racing. Vanderbilt's passion for cars and competition carried him to Europe, where he set a record in 1902 for the distance from Monte Carlo to Paris. Next, he won a match race through the streets of Paris against Baron Henri Rothschild. Inspired to enter the more prestigious and more challenging Gordon Bennett Cup race, precursor to Grand Prix racing, he managed only a lackluster finish.

Vanderbilt retreated to the United States and entered his ninety-horsepower Mercedes in the 1904 races in Daytona. His appearance attracted so many other wealthy entrants that a special race was created for "gentlemen" drivers. Oldfield intruded on this gathering of privilege and European machines with his American-made Bullet no. 2. The premiere mile-long match involved elimination heats. Oldfield and Vanderbilt each won his and advanced to the final, which Oldfield won by a whopping hundred yards. The next day, during a heat of the five-mile event, the crankshaft of his Winton broke. Vanderbilt complained that Oldfield had faked this breakdown in order to deprive him of a reprieve. A special committee was formed to investigate and found that the crankshaft had indeed broken. Although Vanderbilt won all the other races and set new world records for distances from five to fifty miles, his triumph could not check the avalanche of news that the working-class champion had bested the millionaire.[37]

Vanderbilt's loss to Oldfield, his poor performance at Daytona the following year, and his withdrawal from competition heralded a new direction for racing. Henceforth, despite a few notable exceptions, the gentlemen drivers who dominated early racing were muscled off the track and into sponsorship by professionals with more experience, superior skills, and greater determination. When Winton realized that he was no longer good enough to drive his cars and hired Oldfield, he sparked a bit of controversy. The French champion Henri Fournier charged that Barney was being paid to race and maintained that he should not be allowed to compete against drivers who were not.[38] Fournier was perturbed over the collapse of his race against Winton and well aware that European manufacturers were already paying drivers handsomely, but he also knew that Oldfield's contract was a new development for the United States, one that opened a way for a new breed of drivers who raced cars they could not afford to buy and maintain.[39]

Automobile racing is the only professionalized sport covered in this book. Boxing, baseball, and bicycle racing were, of course, exceptions as well. The greater tolerance of professionalization in these sports is not easily explained, but their lower-class constituency supported the participation of their representatives, favored monetary reward, and believed that they deserved it. Even though the concept of amateur remained firmly entrenched during this time and functioned as a barricade against those down the social scale, we have already seen ways in which the unfolding commercialization was undermining the authority of this belief even in upper-class sports like tennis and mountaineering. Automobile racing furnishes an alternative perspective on this commercialization. Money had been so integral to automobile racing from its inception that Oldfield's contract and Fournier's complaint were little noticed and decidedly not the red flag that Reid's salary was. The enormous expense of car racing and its appeal to fugitives from bicycle racing made financing crucial in the earliest races, but surging attendance, which enabled promoters and organizers to pay out fat purses and appearance fees, rapidly escalated this professionalization. If Oldfield's contract elicited little objection, his persistent and resourceful pursuit of financial opportunity eventually affirmed the worst dangers cited by proponents of amateurism.

Oldfield's triumph over Vanderbilt vaulted him to the position of the best-known racer in America. Barney's flamboyance, daring, and victories made the man behind the wheel as important as his machine. Oldfield's working-class background, which initially made automobile racing seem an impossible dream, lured thousands to see him as proof that it could come true. However, ensuing bumps disrupted his neatly orchestrated march to dominance. For a tour of southern events, he jettisoned his agent, Glenn Stuart, and hired Col. "Billy" Thompson. Several weeks into his bookings, Thompson was arrested in New Orleans for intoxication, driving a stolen car, and resisting arrest.[40] Three weeks later the Contest Board of the American Automobile Association disqualified Oldfield for participating in unauthorized races in Atlanta and Birmingham.[41]

32. Barney Oldfield and William Pickens, 1909.
(Oldfield Collection, LA84 Foundation)

This disqualification presented more of a problem than
locating another agent. Only two years old, the AAA was
originally founded to counter widespread hostility toward
motorists and to foster favorable legislation. Hoping to defuse complaints about speeding, it campaigned to restrict
races to regulated venues and drivers approved by its new
Contest Board.[42] As authorized keeper of world records, it
insisted that races have its approval and include one of its
representatives to verify the results.[43] Oldfield's sanction was
one of the Contest Board's first and was issued only because
Thompson's bookings so flagrantly violated the board's rule
that licensed drivers compete only in approved events. Oldfield was so confident that the Contest Board did not have
sufficient support to enforce this decision that he entered and

was allowed to compete in an approved race in Readville, Massachusetts.[44] Wary of adverse publicity from a public confrontation, the board quietly solicited an appeal from Barney for reinstatement and closed the matter.

Winton, on the other hand, was so upset over this sanction and Oldfield's badgering demands for more money that he decided not to renew his contract.[45] Barney immediately persuaded E. A. Moross to be his manager and William Pickens to be his agent. Both men, who would figure prominently in Oldfield's future, negotiated an alternative contract with the Peerless Motor Car Company, Winton's crosstown competitor, and arranged for Barney to retain his current supplement for endorsing Goodrich Tires.

This brazen defiance was fraught with risks, and they surfaced during several losses to Earl Kiser, who was hired by Winton to replace Barney.[46] Fearful that his Peerless Green Dragon might be inferior to Kiser's Bullet, Oldfield resolved to win in Saint Louis and drove so aggressively that he crashed, killed two spectators, and sustained a punctured lung.[47] In his first race following his recovery, he drove cautiously to a disappointing third-place finish. Trusting Barney's resilience, Reeves contracted a rematch at the Empire Track against the Europeans who had beaten him, billed it as "the track championship of the world," and gloated when Barney won.[48]

With Pickens and Moross negotiating his appearances, Oldfield made more money than ever, but he also had to compete in a broader range of races and against stiffer competition, and these pressures altered his outlook on racing. "I'm not in this automobile racing game for my health. It isn't a healthy business," he confessed to the *Los Angeles Times*.

"I'm driving a machine because there's money in it . . . [and] if I wanted to follow the game, I'd do it by proxy—hire some chap to run fast machines. But for the fun there is in it—nix for me."[49]

For Barney money was more important than trophies, honors, or even victories, but this forthright admission suggests that he also had something else on his mind. Crashes were beginning to bother him as much as defeats. He would later explain that the rude, unreliable early cars, which went only fifty to sixty miles an hour, were far more dangerous than their successors, which routinely averaged over a hundred.[50] The year following his Saint Louis crash, Barney again went through a fence at Grosse Pointe. Pressing hard to stay in contention, Barney suddenly lost engine power and was hit from behind. Although no one else was hurt this time, he was knocked unconscious and sent to the hospital with a badly lacerated scalp and a severely bruised right arm. The following week Earl Kiser crushed his leg so badly in a mishap that it had to be amputated. Days later Webb Jay had the worst accident of this fateful August. He was embroiled in a massive collision of cars, caromed off the course, and plunged down a hill into a creek. His skull was fractured, and he sustained so many other serious injuries that everyone believed he would die.[51] Though he did not, his recovery took months, and he never returned to racing. Winton was so upset over the injuries to Kiser and Jay that he withdrew his cars from competition.[52] Peerless summoned Oldfield to Cleveland and afterward announced, "Oldfield will not compete with his Green Dragon in track races."[53] In order to complete his contractual obligations, Oldfield drove his Green Dragon cautiously in a series of exhibitions.

These accidents and their devastating repercussions prompted Oldfield to retire from racing for a role in a Broadway play that made him even more of a celebrity. He agreed to appear in a romantic melodrama titled *The Vanderbilt Cup* (1906), which utilized the best-known race of the era as an occasion for singing, socializing, and love. The same year that William K. Vanderbilt first competed at Daytona, he established the Vanderbilt Cup as an international competition in order to attract premiere racers from Europe and to spur American manufacturers to build better machines. Although this multicar road race attracted crowds over one hundred thousand by its second year, Oldfield had not participated in this event and would not do so until years later. The play's thrilling climax presented him triumphing over another car — an enactment that resembled his two-car matches more than the multicar Vanderbilt event, especially with Tom Cooper ensconced in the car that Oldfield was beating. "Fine Racing Effect," proclaimed the headline of the review in the *New York Times*.[54] The ironies emanating from this frivolous contrivance were compounded when Cooper was killed in a car accident in Central Park after a late night of carousing.[55] Next, the two hundred thousand plus spectators who flocked to the Vanderbilt Cup later that year so increased the potential for accidents and injuries that the race was immediately discontinued (for only a year, it turned out).

"Why don't I go into the Vanderbilt cup races?" Oldfield replied to a curious reporter. "Nothing would give me greater pleasure, but when I do enter that race I want a car that has some chance to win." He explained that Europeans cared more for racing, crafted superior vehicles, and paid their drivers better.[56] Prior to his Grosse Pointe accident, Oldfield had pressed Peerless to build him an improved racer, but the company was so sensitive to the increasing expense and danger that it balked.[57] When Barney finally wearied of *The Vanderbilt Cup* and returned to racing, he decided against manufacturer affiliation and sponsorship. Instead, he reconnected with Moross, and they purchased cars of their own. Upset by the caution of American carmakers and the numerous crashes, Oldfield decided that he needed more control over his races. An initial acquisition of a Peerless Green Dragon no. 3 and a Blue Streak, followed by an addition of two Stearns a year later, kept Barney abreast of current developments, patriotically loyal to American products, and best of all, ringmaster of his events.[58] Over the course of replacing older vehicles with new ones, Moross contracted drivers for the fading ones or sold them to drivers willing to appear in Barney's shows. He also understood that transportation was a major factor in budgeting and that the cost for several cars was not much greater than that for one. Best of all, multiple cars empowered Moross to negotiate favorable fees and dates with race organizers, often providing an entire slate of races for fair-like events. Over time this strategy evolved into barnstorming entourages of automobiles and drivers and led inevitably to charges that Oldfield's races were rigged.[59]

Racing's consequential loss of credibility soon outstripped the complaints about injuries and deaths. The Manufacturers Contest Association (MCA) had long been a powerful ally of the AAA, and at its annual convention in 1908, this problem generated heated discussion. Reluctant to overstep his jurisdiction, MCA chairman H. E. Coffin relayed this concern to L. R. Speare, president of the AAA, who perceived daunting potholes in the road to reform. Local clubs wanted the national organization to coordinate scheduling and authenticate records but coveted sponsorship of their races and complained vigorously if their wishes and needs were not respected. Ever since his original disqualification, Oldfield understood how this conflict worked to his advantage, as locals consistently favored headliners who drew crowds over stronger regulation and enforcement.

Speare saw his priority as upholding the AAA's original mission of strengthening the national organization and helping motorists. Thus he channeled his initiative into a campaign for a national highway (the Lincoln Highway), a set of accurate road maps, and a reliable guide to accommodations. He delegated responsibility for racing to Frank Hower and a reconstituted Contest Board. "Up to this point, the Contest Board, like all other self-proclaimed sanctioning bodies, had been something of a joke," auto historian Russ Catlin has aptly characterized the situation facing Hower. "There was no way that sanctioners could enforce their rules, suspensions or fines. Drivers laughed at their efforts and jumped at will from one organization to another, seeking the most lucrative races or the most appearance money." Hower made his first objective an alliance between the AAA and the elitist Automobile Club of America (ACA). As a condition of his successful brokerage of this marriage, he agreed to be succeeded by Sam Butler, the long-standing secretary of the ACA, who advocated establishment of an exclusive slate of "national" events that would include both the Vanderbilt Cup and the Grand Prize, which had previously been controlled by the ACA.[60]

This ingenious plan simply ignored the myriad smaller races that were impossible to police, advocated a consolidation already resulting from ruinous competition, and garnered the Contest Board more authority.[61] The events on this new slate would attract the best competition, feature the finest cars, vault them to premiere status, and enable them to offer the largest purses. These races would be more important than any single driver, and everyone hoping to participate would have to comply with the Control Board's regulations. Needless to say, successful implementation of this plan necessitated skillful statesmanship.

The plethora of events that spurred this initiative kept Ralph De Palma from racing Oldfield over most of his own meteoric ascent to stardom. De Palma came to the United States from Italy at nine years old and bypassed school to work in a bicycle shop. Like Oldfield he was a disgruntled worker who turned to bicycle racing as possible liberation but transitioned quickly to automobiles. His association with a garage earned him an invitation to chauffeur for the Vanderbilt family and introduced him to several wealthy car enthusiasts, including Frederick Moskovics. When Moskovics became general manager of the Allen Kingston Motor Company, he hired De Palma to assemble and test his cars.[62] In the spring of 1908 Moskovics allowed De Palma to drive one of his cars at a Fort George Hill Climb. In Readville De Palma won his first race and took second in a five-mile event that Oldfield won. Barney's snubbing of De Palma afterward may have originated their lifelong hostility toward each other.[63]

Weeks after Readville, Emanuel Cedrino, the lead driver for Fiat's United States team, was killed at Pimlico. De Palma

33. Ralph De Palma, 1912.
(Chicago History Museum, photograph by the *Chicago Daily News*, SDN 057946)

was hired to replace him, and he quickly capitalized on this position to better records that Oldfield had held for years. These successes fueled speculation that Oldfield was about to challenge De Palma and reclaim his records.[64]

After several unexceptional years in American cars, Oldfield decided that he needed to reduce his barnstorming, acquire a foreign car, and revive his flagging reputation. When

David Bruce-Brown crashed his 120-horsepower Benz at a hill climb in June 1909, Oldfield and Moross moved quickly to acquire the car.[65] Mercedes had originally developed this Victor Hémery prototype for the French Grand Prix, entered two of them in the 1908 Grand Prize in Savannah, and allowed Bruce-Brown to purchase one afterward. The *New York Times'* announcement of Barney's purchase perceptively observed: "Since the Peerless Green Dragon went out of date, the irrepressible Barney has had no car with which he could compete against specially built racers, such as the [Fiat] Cyclone and the Christie."[66]

Oldfield's purpose-built Benz racer was hastily repaired for an upcoming event in Indianapolis. Carl Fisher was developing the future site of the 500 and had arranged for Moross to become his director of contests. Barney's lucrative agreement to compete there may have facilitated acquisition of his Benz, and he used his purchase to recover several records, including one recently set by De Palma for the oval mile.[67]

Well before Barney's refurbished Benz finished a half lap ahead of De Palma's Cyclone in Indianapolis, everyone associated with Fiat's team knew that the company needed a faster car to maintain its dominance. A new 200-horsepower Mephistopheles had already demonstrated its enormous potential at the new Brooklands track in England, and De Palma had arranged to have it for a heavily advertised ten-mile event in Atlanta, which had also booked Oldfield with his Benz and Walter Christie with his new car. Unfortunately, De Palma broke his thigh bone in a Danbury race, and Lewis Strang had to replace him.[68] Strang piloted the Mephistopheles to such a commanding lead over Oldfield and Christie that he slowed through the final lap and still bettered Oldfield's recent Indianapolis record.[69]

This defeat was not the setback for Oldfield that it may have appeared. He knew about the formidable Mephistopheles and was already negotiating for an even more powerful Mercedes. Barney's return to serious racing was influenced by contracts from Moross in Indianapolis and an ensuing reunion with his former agent, William Pickens. Pickens had been managing Buick's racing team, which won many races in 1909, but he and several of his drivers, including Strang, abruptly quit in late summer. A newspaper report of this shake-up, which predated Strang's victory in Atlanta, stated that Pickens was traveling to Europe to secure a new 200-horsepower Benz for Oldfield.[70]

Months before Pickens sailed for Europe, he knew that Daytona was losing money on its races and was in danger of folding if attendance did not improve the following spring. Meanwhile, New Orleans was preparing a major event for the week of Mardi Gras, and a new board track, the first of its kind, was scheduled to open a month later in Los Angeles. Before Pickens took ownership of the expensive Benz, which he named Blitzen and later converted to its English translation, Lightning, he approached organizers of these venues with an offer of Barney and his new car for a substantial percentage of the gate.

Pickens also realized that his client's participation in these events would increase the value of his endorsements. For the past three years Oldfield had been loyally voicing his satisfaction with Goodyear tires, but Pickens converted him to Firestone for higher compensation and coverage of his substantial transportation costs. Several weeks into this new

34. Freight car for Oldfield's automobiles, 1910.

(Ed Wallen)

contract, Oldfield remarked to reporters that he had allowed his life insurance to lapse and was currently unable to obtain a renewal.[71] Firestone marketing staff speedily reconfigured this revelation into "Firestone tires—my only insurance," painted the quote on his race cars, and featured it in ads.

The centerpiece of this aggressive promotion was Pickens's orchestration of his southern tour so that each stop included a contest between Oldfield and De Palma in their imposing automobiles. When Barney tried to enter his first Benz in a race in Philadelphia's Fairmont Park, officials ruled that it was not a "stock" car and barred it.[72] The "stock" limitation had long been a cornerstone of American racing and was intended to stimulate sales of the commercial product and to prevent specially designed racers from dominating events. However, recent production of purpose-built racers—the new Mercedes and Fiat models in Europe along with the American Christie—challenged this restriction and led to what Gary Doyle has aptly characterized as "the swan song of the stock car."[73] Crowds no longer turned out simply to see races; they wanted ones comprised of the newest, fastest, most powerful machines. The organizers in Atlanta understood this attraction and created a special match for purpose-built machines, which Pickens sought to replicate during Barney's tour.

De Palma's injury, which kept him out of the competition in Atlanta, disrupted Pickens's cunning (and false) promotion of this race as an initial reckoning of the two champions. Undaunted, he simply passed his hyped billing of the two to the next event and stoked even greater anticipation.[74] However, a truly unbelievable sequence of mechanical breakdowns plagued these matches.

Halfway through the first lap of his race against De Palma in New Orleans, Oldfield abruptly slowed his Blitzen and left the track complaining about a problem with its gearing.[75] No further explanation was provided. At Daytona Barney drew a huge crowd for his attempt at the fastest straightaway mile, and he pushed his Blitzen to an eye-popping speed of 131.72 miles per hour.[76] But again his much-anticipated battle against De Palma evaporated. The announcement this time—that the Fiat had developed a cracked piston—was less persuasive because a full week before, a local newspaper had reported that the event would be canceled "since the bottoms fell out of several alleged 'purses.'"[77] A much longer account in another paper likewise furnished advance notice of this cancellation and a revelation that a contractual agreement between Pickens and the race organizers granted Oldfield exclusive rights to the speed events and barred De Palma from participating in them. This news prompted an angry telegram from New York instructing De Palma to quit the Oldfield race and ship the Mephistopheles back there immediately.[78]

Oldfield's abrupt exit from the track in New Orleans may

have involved a purse problem there too. Afterward De Palma was so annoyed over what happened that he complained to reporters, "I don't believe in hippodroming. Promoters have offered me large sums of money to go barnstorming around the country with three or four second-raters, whom I could beat every time with ease—after the fashion of a certain well-known track driver. I want to see the game on a legitimate basis. I have always found that I could win my share without 'hiring and maintaining a string of dubs.'"[79] The breakdown of Oldfield's car in New Orleans and De Palma's cracked piston at Daytona left racing fans wondering if the two rivals would ever compete against each other, but Pickens moved quickly to explain that they indeed would, reaffirming the purse for their upcoming match at the new Motordrome in Los Angeles and using it to appease De Palma's offended backers.[80] But once again Pickens was slyly dealing from a stacked deck: he had secretly negotiated a contract that awarded the winner one thousand of the five-thousand-dollar guarantee, and Oldfield was to receive the remaining four thousand dollars as an appearance fee.[81]

The mandated return of Mephistopheles to New York and belated approval for it to race in Del Rey caused it to arrive late for trial runs. Two days before the race, the big Fiat developed another cracked piston and was withdrawn.[82] Pickens scrambled to replace the much-publicized, much-anticipated match between Oldfield and De Palma with a three-heat event involving Barney in his Blitzen against Caleb Bragg in a Fiat Cyclone. Oldfield unwisely agreed to a stationary start, which left the much heavier Benz spinning its wheels as the fleet Cyclone bolted to a commanding lead and easily won the first two heats. Bragg's amateur status made his victory huge, but it also blocked him from accepting prize money and sent the entire purse to Oldfield and Pickens.[83]

These aborted races generated substantial disappointment and an awkward problem for the Contest Board of the AAA. Samuel Butler, its new head, attended the opening of the Motordrome as a gesture of good will. He possessed both an insider's knowledge of the recent string of race cancellations and a solid understanding of the board's rules, which required licensed drivers to honor their commitments. He was also wise enough to realize that any application of this rule to Oldfield or De Palma could be explosive. His goal was to build support for racing and to avoid ruinous controversy.

As much as Butler objected to Oldfield's relentless quest for money, publicity, and his own way, he needed a more flagrant violation to move against the people's champion. Three months later Oldfield announced that he had agreed to race Jack Johnson, the black heavyweight boxing champion and recent winner over Jim Jeffries, "the great white hope." Johnson, who loved fast cars, was emboldened by his victory to challenge Oldfield. Since Jeffries was a close friend, Oldfield considered the proposal an opportunity for reprisal, but his chief motive remained the same. "Automobile racing is my business," he explained in a press release, "and if Johnson or any other man in the world has $5,000 to bet he can beat me at my game I am ready to race."[84] Johnson neither bet nor posted five thousand dollars, but his celebrity status enabled Pickens to market the race to the Sheepshead Bay Track outside New York City and to contract its film rights with Hollywood.

These contingency agreements involved risk, but none

approached that of Oldfield's outright violation of the Contest Board's rules against licensed professionals competing
against drivers without credentials and racing experience.
When the date of the race was announced, the Contest Board
issued an announcement that the race would not be sanc-
tioned and that Johnson's improperly obtained license had
been revoked. The *New York Times'* account of this news
included a Butler statement that "competition of this sort
would not do the sport any good" and that "the governing
board of this organization would not stand for such a race."
The *New York Herald Tribune* spiced its report with a Pickens quote: "Oldfield is bigger than the AAA Contest Board."
When Butler read this comment, he convened an emergency
board meeting and secured approval for a motion, timed to
appear in newspapers the next morning, which declared that
Oldfield had been "suspended and disqualified until further
notice."[85] Barney calmly left for an approved race in Readville, Massachusetts, as he did during his first disqualification. Afterward he told reporters, "To win my first battle
with the American Automobile Association in the home of
its President and with him on the track is one of the greatest
victories of my life."[86] The Contest Board countered this brazen defiance with an announcement that Oldfield's suspension would be "indefinite" and include his cars.[87]

Oldfield easily won his ensuing race against Johnson, but
its tepid receipts were an ominous harbinger of costly consequences. When he returned to Atlanta for another approved
race, he was turned away and his legal appeal for redress of
twenty thousand dollars was denied.[88] In California the only
venue willing to accept him was the renegade Ascot track.
Daytona and Indianapolis sided with the AAA and barred

him from upcoming events. Amid preparations for the Indianapolis 500, Carl Fisher announced: "Oldfield will never set another tire on these bricks."[89]

This wall of opposition sent Oldfield back into retirement. With the AAA and the major venues united against him, his best prospect was to apologize to the Contest Board, appeal his suspension, and comply with its rules. But he refused. The other option was barnstorming fairs and secondary events, but under current conditions this was a sure route to oblivion. Barney's predicament provoked a characterization of himself to the press as a beleaguered entrepreneur and endangered species:

> I have a lot of money invested in racing. . . . No other race driver in the world makes a business of racing. That is, no other driver owns his own racing cars, a traveling railway garage, maintains a complete race promoting force and races on a percentage of the receipts, taking a financial as well as physical chance instead of for prizes. I am the only driver in the world who has no factory affiliation, no axes to grind with sundry manufacturers, and no interest of any sort in the trade. Consequently, rules that are accepted and followed by other drivers cannot be accepted and followed by me.[90]

He hoped this explanation would rally support, but it did more to justify his sanction. The Contest Board was campaigning for legitimate events and intent on making them more important than individual drivers, especially ones with agendas like this.

E. A. Moross, Oldfield's former manager and current director of contests in Indianapolis, understood why his boss,

35. "Hard Luck" Ralph De Palma at the second
Indianapolis 500, 1912.
(IMPS photo, Indianapolis Motor Speedway)

Earl Fisher, stonewalled Barney, but he also pined for his
old job. When he learned that Oldfield was leaving racing
to open a bar, he acquired his fleet of cars, successfully appealed the Contest Board's sanction against them, and gathered talented drivers for them. As Barney passed the spring
of 1911 welcoming patrons to his new tavern in Los Angeles,
Moross tapped Jim Burman to drive the Blitzen at Daytona,
and he bettered Oldfield's speed record from the year before
by almost ten miles per hour.

Adversity likewise stalked De Palma and brought him
the nickname "Hard Luck Ralph." "De Palma's Hoodoo
Again," the *New York Times* headlined its account of his
second cracked piston.[91] Later that year at the Grand Prize

race in Savannah, De Palma had an insurmountable lead going into the penultimate lap when a rock flew up from the
track, penetrated his radiator, and forced him out of the race.
At the first Indianapolis 500 in 1911, he finished a dispiriting
sixth. He met with even greater disappointment the following year when his car, again with a commanding lead that he
had sustained for 194 laps, faltered and subsequently broke
down in the backstretch of the penultimate lap. Perhaps the
most famous photograph from all 500s is that of De Palma
and his mechanic vainly pushing their doomed vehicle. Later
that same year, during the final lap of the Grand Prize he
attempted to pass Caleb Bragg, who held the lead. The ensuing collision caused De Palma to crash and hospitalized
him with a punctured abdomen. Fortunately, victories out-
numbered these setbacks. In 1912 he won the Elgin Trophy,
a free-for-all at Santa Monica, and finally the prestigious
Vanderbilt Cup. Although today's system of points was not
initiated until a decade later, two of the best-known car
magazines named De Palma that year's champion.[92]

Racing had problems as well. Although crowds still
flocked to major events, they were less dependable. The efforts of organizers to revive the Vanderbilt Cup and Grand
Prize races by moving them to Savannah succeeded initially
and then faltered. Waning attendance at Fairmont Park, the
Los Angeles Motordrome, and Atlanta spurred the Contest
Board to transfer these premiere events to Milwaukee for
1912. Bad crashes and the shocking death of Bruce-Brown
intensified the problems of the races and led to suspension of
them for the next year.

When William C. Schimpf became head of the Contest
Board, selection of an appropriate site for resumption of

the races was critical, and upheaval in California worsened the situation. When Oldfield fled to California to escape his sanction, he understood that the Los Angeles area had both a unique enthusiasm for auto racing and a chauvinistic suspicion of the AAA. He tried unsuccessfully to rally locals against his disqualification by characterizing himself as an "outlaw" battling a snobbish eastern tyrant.[93] This estimate won belated support when a petty feud erupted between Schimpf and California officials and he slapped them with suspensions. This affront sparked claims that the AAA was dominated by midwestern manufacturers and fueled a move to have the Western Automobile Association replace it and develop its own slate of races. Fearful that this unfolding storm could devastate all that the AAA and its Contest Board had been working so hard to accomplish, Schimpf sought peace by awarding both races to Santa Monica for 1914. However, the negotiations were so contentious and stressful, he resigned as soon as the agreement was signed.[94]

Both Oldfield and De Palma agreed to participate in the 1914 Vanderbilt Cup, but the evolution of their careers since cancellation of the Motordrome race had deepened their long-standing antagonism. Hoping that Oldfield's popularity might counter the worrisome drop in attendance, Schimpf ended his suspension three months early, but Barney was unable to resume where he had left off.[95] He had sold his cars and could no longer afford to replace them. He was only able to participate in that year's Grand Prize because Bruce-Brown's death in the Vanderbilt Cup event left the owner of his quickly repaired Mercedes in need of a driver. Forced to attend the Indianapolis 500 for 1913 as a spectator, he purchased a used Christie there and successfully used it at Daytona to reclaim his speed record from Burman. However, this discounted rocket was too unwieldy for the increasingly popular road races. In the races that followed, Oldfield had to drive cars someone else owned. His unfamiliarity with them, and perhaps their lack of potential, produced middling results.

Meanwhile, the Mercer Automobile Company invited De Palma to be head of its racing team. Its recent victories on the race circuit spurred development of a purpose-built Type 45. De Palma provided valuable input during construction and with mechanical problems in the finished product. Its initial burst of success attracted George Settle, a wealthy car enthusiast from Southern California, who purchased one for Oldfield to drive. In it Barney nearly won a Santa Monica race but squandered his commanding lead by taking a curve at excessive speed; this recklessness caused him to blow two tires, which knocked him out of the race. He pushed his Mercer to another late lead at Corona, but a young boy who wandered on the track necessitated a violent swerve and caused a crash that cost him this race as well.[96]

These showings brought Oldfield an invitation to join the Mercer team. Justifiably offended by this clandestine move and callous disregard for someone who had been so loyal and invested so much, De Palma resigned. Suddenly the characteristic positions of both drivers were reversed. Oldfield, who had not signed a contract with a manufacturer since Peerless, was for the first time affiliated with a company team. De Palma, who had been with teams most of his career, was now on his own. In order to participate in the upcoming Vanderbilt Cup, he had to persuade Edward J. Schroeder to loan him back the Grey Ghost Mercedes that he had driven to victory in several major races over the past two years. This abrupt turnabout gained Oldfield *the* hot, new car, the one his rival had developed and was supposed to drive, and left De Palma in one widely believed to be over the hill.

Local newspapers covering the upcoming Vanderbilt Cup announced that De Palma and Oldfield would be "settling a grudge" but did not delve into the reasons for it. Unseasonably heavy rains pushed back the originally scheduled date, but careful preparation, elaborate promotion, and much-improved weather brought a huge turnout. Robert S. Firestone, brother of the founder of the Firestone Tire Company, came from distant Ohio to cheer Barney.[97] Firestone had loyally supported Oldfield through his suspension and even offered him a position with the company. When he returned to racing, Firestone's ads again trumpeted his endorsement of its tires, and Robert came to the race expecting him to drive on them to victory.

De Palma realized that his burly Mercedes would have difficulty staying with Oldfield's fleet, nimble Mercer through the thirty-five twisting laps of the 8.4-mile course. His best hope was to maintain his speed, easing through the tight curves as smoothly as possible, and unleash the power of his Ghost in the straightaways. Since Oldfield was likely to stress his tires as he always had, most recently at Santa Monica, De Palma planned to pressure his tires as little as possible and hoped to complete the 294-mile race without having to change them.[98]

Early in the race Eddie Pullen pushed another Mercer into a commanding lead, but a burst tire and a spectacular crash during the thirteenth lap sent his car out of the

36. Ralph De Palma (*left*) and Barney Oldfield during
Vanderbilt Cup in Santa Monica, 1914.

(Oldfield Collection LA84 Foundation)

race. De Palma moved into second place following Pullen's
elimination and took over the lead five laps later. Oldfield,
who had already stopped twice, was a minute behind and
determined to catch up. Steadily over the next six laps, he
successfully narrowed the gap to eight seconds but did not
try for the lead. Seemingly confident that his Mercer could
pass the Mercedes whenever he elected, he closed and then
dropped back, patiently waiting for the perfect moment. But
it never came. The outcome of the race was decided four
laps from the finish when Oldfield pulled over for a final
tire change. During an earlier lap, De Palma's mechanic had
signaled for a stop, but Ralph did not do so. For years stories circulated that this was a ruse and that it successfully
snookered Oldfield into stopping, but George Hill, who was

accompanying Barney, later swore that a tire puncture compelled his partner to stop. Moreover, the signal from De Palma's mechanic was only meant to ready the crew *in case* the Ghost had to pull over.[99] It is also possible that Oldfield divined De Palma's strategy much earlier and realized the costliness of his tire changes. His earlier pit stops necessitated that he push his Mercer to *average* two to four miles an hour faster than the Ghost just to keep up. Thus Oldfield held back in order to conserve his tires, avoid more stops, and wait until late in the race to pass, but the failure of his Firestone ended this nerve-wracking duel and awarded the victory to De Palma.

From its inception, automobile racing has been perhaps *the* most commercialized of all sports, and the reason for this is quite simple: race cars are very expensive and so too their development and maintenance. On the other hand, people have always been so captivated by the power and speed of automobiles that they have willingly paid large amounts to watch them compete. Barney Oldfield understood this correlation of cost and appeal from the moment he drove the rude 999 onto the track at Grosse Pointe in 1902. There he demonstrated that the skill and personality of the driver were equally important to attracting crowds. He and his agents resourcefully capitalized on appearance fees, endorsements, and purses to achieve lucrative returns, but their shrewd management of this risky business steered racing toward staged events and away from the serious competition so crucial to the sport's future.

The revitalized Contest Board of the AAA, the appearance of purpose-built machines, and the emergence of Ralph De Palma as the new champion of regulated racing pressured

Oldfield to change, but not enough to save him from a devastating disqualification. Barney's return to racing and participation in the 1914 Vanderbilt Cup contributed greatly to the high stakes of that race. The event itself was a major victory for the A A A's resurgent Contest Board. Its outcome was also a gratifying vindication of De Palma's brilliant planning and fervent commitment to serious racing. However, his vehement objection to Barney's fixation with monetary return also left De Palma scarred. Over the years that followed, he adamantly refused to use Firestone tires, even though more and more drivers were converting to them. His nephew, a member of his racing crew, eventually quit because he believed that his uncle's irrational opposition to Firestone was costing him victories.[100]

Epilogue

In a poem titled "Alumnus Football," first published in 1908, Grantland Rice memorably wrote, "For when the one Great Scorer comes to write against your name, He marks—not that you won or lost—but how you played the game."[1] Although these words are still fondly remembered, at the time when Rice wrote them, long before the 1920s, which made both him and his couplet famous, he was speaking out on behalf of an entrenched belief. For years early proponents of sport had been arguing that the recently developed games were supposed to be recreation and a therapeutic alternative to work. According to this philosophy play mattered and the outcome didn't. Participants were encouraged to value the benefits of physical exertion and social interaction over the final score.

However, Rice's support for this ethic was tinged with awareness that it was endangered. He understood that by 1908 athletic events had already evolved into serious competitions quite different from the rude skirmishes they once were. Indeed, winning had grown very important to an ever-expanding range of enthusiasts. The players who were currently training long and hard for events, the entrepreneurs who were arranging and promoting them, the crowds who were purchasing costly tickets for them, and the journalists, like himself, who were capitalizing on them for livelihoods affirmed that a tectonic shift had occurred and propelled sport beyond the wildest dreams of its earliest supporters.

Martina Navratilova would spotlight our age's distance from Rice's view of sport with her observation: "Whoever said, it's not whether you win or lose, probably lost." The chapters of this book likewise stray from Rice's maxim with their close accounting of wins and losses. Most were neither memorable nor important enough to be engraved alongside the names of my athletes in any grand tome of sport. In this quite different accounting, they are more like checkpoint measures in the development of their careers. But some victories do indeed stand out and legitimately warrant being remembered — and so too a few crushing defeats incurred along the way. Nevertheless, these profiles do emulate Rice's standard in focusing on how these champions "played" during this seminal period of sport's evolution into strenuous commercialized competition.

Rice believed that playing well involved those long-esteemed traits of being vigorous and amicable, playing wisely, and abiding by the rules. Above all Rice believed that players should be good sports. Although the figures of this book were indoctrinated with these expectations, they were exceptionally driven to win and/or succeed, and being a good sport was well down their list of priorities. Frequently, their drive was so intense that it made them offensive and unlikable, but it also carried them to the forefront of their sports and contributed to the development of momentous events. If their intent on victory and recognition made them formidable adversaries, it also alerted them to the escalating importance of money and organizations. They either shrewdly grasped or painfully learned that these sideline considerations were as essential to their success as their athletic prowess. These imposing obstacles had to be assessed and engaged as carefully as any of their opponents. Money, of course, was an advantage—and a necessity; either you had it, or you had to get it. The widespread support for amateurism privileged the wealthy, who could pay for their needs, but the surging interest in sport opened up opportunities for the needy to access funding, so long as they did so without pocketing direct payments. This potentially menacing minefield was either defused or worsened by the expanding authority of supervisory organizations. They and their supporters could provide financing to a person with promise or punish anyone who obtained it improperly. Moreover, they decided how the sport was to be conducted, developed a uniform set of rules, amended them as warranted, and assumed responsibility for their enforcement. These circumstances pressured these early combatants to realize that they were, in fact, involved in two games: the one in which they were competing and the one against these outside forces.[2] Moreover, these dual games necessitated that they recognize the special challenges of each and develop effective strategies for both. Although this fuller record reveals that these early champions were not so successful against these outside forces, it deepens our understanding of their substantial contribution to the evolution of sport.

Acknowledgments

Each day I am amazed how much my research is facilitated by the ever-expanding universe of today's Internet. More and more newspapers, journals, books, and photographs are becoming available online, and they are accompanied by constantly improving tools for identifying and isolating the information they can provide. Indeed, this book would be quite different had I been relying on the same methods of research that I was employing only several years back.

Nonetheless, the best memories of my research come from my experiences and especially the many generous individuals who helped me along the way. Although my interest in the history of sport originated with the courses I taught in American studies, my commitment to this project was cemented by an early research trip to California funded by a Haynes grant from the Historical Society of Southern California. Although I had at the time only topical interests and vague plans, I was grateful for this initial support, which proved invaluable in narrowing the focus my investigation and reassuring me of the promise of my selections. This trip carried me to the Southern Regional Library at UCLA and the Los Angeles Public Library, where I found a wealth of material about tennis. At the LA84 Foundation, Mike Salmon provided superb guidance to its resources on automobile racing. My assessment of these findings was greatly aided by enlightening feedback from Gary Doyle, Tony Thacher, and Gordon Sabine. Susan Painter at the Serra Research Center of the San Diego Public Library, Grace Prentiss at the Pasadena Public Library, and Kit Willis at the Ventura Historical Society later located and mailed me important material from their collections.

The gratifying results of my California trip were enriched by ensuing visits to the Harvard Archives, Yale's Archives and Manuscripts, and the U.S. Tennis Hall of Fame, in Newport, Rhode Island, where Mark Young directed me to more nuggets than I ever expected. The Hagley Museum, in Wilmington, Delaware, and especially the Free Library of Philadelphia proved to be invaluable resources for rare books and obscure journals. The Free Library possesses a vast collection of rare materials that are quickly retrieved for the user. The City of Philadelphia is currently coping with acute budget problems, and I hope it can find a way to sustain this unique resource. The University of Delaware Library was an enormous help with its interlibrary loan, its media services (especially Bryce Spencer), and my research study. Commodore Joseph at the MacRobert Trust, Olive Geddes at the National Library of Scotland, Edinburgh, Ron McQueeny at the Indianapolis Speedway, and Ed Wallen at Wallen Racing Classics, in Glendale, Arizona, were sorely pressed with other demands, but graciously found time for mine. I also want to thank David Slovak, who helped enormously with preparation of my photographs.

The writing of this book took longer and proved to be more taxing than I ever anticipated, and I am very grateful for the encouragement and suggestions of several colleagues at the University of Delaware: Jerry Beasley, Kevin Kerrane, Steve Bernhardt, and George Basalla. When individual trees confuse your sense of the forest, it is helpful to have friends willing to help you out.

Robert Taylor at the University of Nebraska Press gave me a final boost with his strong interest in this project, his helpful advice, and his conscientious responsiveness to my inquiries.

Most of all, I want to thank my patient, understanding wife, who kept reminding me that writing a book should be only a part of life.

Notes

Introduction

1. Oriard, *King Football*, 25.

2. Fountain, *Sportswriter*, 162; Evensen, *When Dempsey Fought Tunney*, 30.

3. Evensen, *When Dempsey Fought Tunney*, ix–x.

4. Fountain, *Sportswriter*, 228.

5. Fountain, *Sportswriter*, 45.

6. Quoted in Inabinett, *Grantland Rice and His Heroes*, 20.

7. Fountain, *Sportswriter*, 58–62.

8. Mott, *History of American Magazines*, 3:635–36.

9. Levine, *Spalding and the Rise of Baseball*, 75–84; Hardy, "Adopted by All the Leading Clubs," 133–50.

10. In his theoretical discussion of the distinctions between modern sports and their historical antecedents, Alan Guttmann lists several other important traits that would have radically altered my narrative had I tried to treat them as well. See Guttmann, *From Ritual to Record*.

11. Rader, *American Sports*, 72–76. For a fuller discussion of amateurism, see Pope, *Patriotic Games*, 6–7, 19–53. Pope points out that amateurism was a new concept that developed in the United States and England over the last quarter of the nineteenth century and was from the beginning destabilized by inherent contradictions.

1. Tom Stevens

1. *Boston Daily Globe*, August 5, 1884, 1.

2. Stevens, *Around the World on a Bicycle*, 2 vols. (New York: Scribner's, 1887–88). Ensuing references to this edition will be cited parenthetically within the text and the notes.

3. The exact date of Stevens's departure from Missouri for the West has never been determined, but the early photograph of him on p. 5 comes from a shop in St. Louis and carries the date of 1878. Consequently he must have left after this date.

4. This point was frequently mentioned in newspaper accounts about his trip and was validated by Lyman Bagg (Karl Kron), who knew Stevens and is perhaps the most reliable source of biographical information about him. He wrote, "He had never even mounted a wheel, at the time of conceiving this idea." Bagg, *10,000 Miles on a Bicycle*, 474. Another important source of biographical information on Stevens is "Outing's Portrait Gallery: Thomas Stevens," 183–85. Irving Leonard has offered valuable background on Stevens in his *First across America*. Leonard has also written a series of helpful, informative articles on Stevens for *Wheelmen* magazine. A complete bibliography of these can be found in its special issue on Stevens. *Wheelmen*, May 1984, 8.

5. A sketch of Stevens, published just following his ride across the country, mentioned seven previously unsuccessful efforts. *Harper's Weekly*, August 30, 1884, 563.

6. "History on the Go!," 17–18.

7. During his ride through Nebraska, Stevens commented: "I consider it a lucky day that passes without adding one or more to my long and eventful list of headers" (1:73).

8. *Chicago Daily Times Herald*, July 5, 1884, 3. Also Bagg, *10,000 Miles on a Bicycle*, 475. When Stevens reached England with his fancier Columbia Expert, he had it outfitted with a custom-made box for his writing materials (1:97). In this he also put medical supplies, a can of oil, and underclothing. He also carried

a tent that he wrapped around the frame so as to include extra spokes and a spare tire (1:251).

9. This experience is only summarized in Stevens's book, but he offered a much fuller account in a letter to *Outing* magazine that was his first publication about his trip. See Stevens, "Bicycling in the Far West," *Outing and the Wheelman*, September 1884, 463–64.

10. "Bicycle-Making," 2.

11. Pope, "Colonel Albert A. Pope's Response," 70.

12. "Bicycle-Making," 2–5. Also Pope, "Colonel Albert A. Pope's Response," 70–71.

13. Pope, "Colonel Albert A. Pope's Response," 69. Additional information about Pope and his company can be found in Goddard, *Colonel Albert Pope*, 66–88; Leonard, "Colonel Albert A. Pope," 7–8; Geist, "American Bicycle Hall of Fame," 29.

14. Pope, "Colonel Albert A. Pope's Response," 71.

15. Wells, "Sunrise in America," 3, 9. A *Harper's* article on bicycles, which drew heavily on Pratt's *American Bicycler* (1879), described Pratt as "the president of the League of American Wheelmen, and a lawyer by profession, who has in his work made a careful study from the records of the patent offices, both of Europe and this country, of the steps by which the bicycle has been brought to its present perfection." Howland, "Bicycle Era," 282.

16. Quoted in Howland, "Bicycle Era," 285.

17. Wells, "Sunrise in America," 3, 9. See also Pratt, "Wheel around the Hub Tour," 481–99.

18. Mott, *History of American Magazines*, 4:633.

19. "Bicycle-Making," 4.

20. *Chicago Daily Times Herald*, July 5, 1884, 3.

21. Leonard, "Thomas Stevens," 8; *Outing and the Wheelman*, September 1884, 463–64.

22. *Boston Post*, August 5, 1884, 5.

23. *Boston Daily Globe*, August 5, 1884, 1. This account likewise mentions Stevens "fifty-inch Standard Columbia bicycle."

24. "Outing's Portrait Gallery" notes Stevens's failure to secure the funding he needed for continuation of his trip, 184. Bagg reports more specifically: "Col. Pope then presented him with a nickeled Expert, in exchange for the old machine, but made no further motion to encourage a continuation." Bagg, *10,000 Miles on a Bicycle*, 474.

25. Quoted in Howland, "Bicycle Era," 285.

26. *San Francisco Chronicle*, January, 8, 1887, 2.

27. Leonard, "Thomas Stevens," 9.

28. *Boston Daily Globe*, August 10, 1884, 8.

29. *Outing*, May 1887, 186, my italics.

30. Bagg, *10,000 Miles on a Bicycle*, 474.

31. *Wheelman* was published in Boston, and *Outing* came from Albany. During the year of their consolidation, the editorial offices were established in New York City.

32. Bagg says Stevens could not find an American publisher for this manuscript. He is unsure whether Stevens took it with him to London or left it in the United States with plans of incorporating it into his book about the entire trip. Bagg, *10,000 Miles On a Bicycle*, 474. Whatever the case, Stevens's substantial reduction of this material in his articles and book means that a much fuller record of his American trip might exist if indeed his manuscript does. His compression of his dramatic Omaha letter into a short informational paragraph in the book (1:58) leaves one wondering how much other interesting material he might have left out.

33. *Outing and the Wheelman*, November 1884, 161.

34. *Outing and the Wheelman*, March 1885, 481.

35. See *New York Times*, October 3, 1885, 3; November 29, 1888, 2; January 16, 1886, 2; May 16, 1886, 14; May 18, 1886, 5; July 8, 1886, 3; August 23, 1886, 5; August 31, 1886, 8; December 14, 1886, 12; December 16, 1886, 5; December 26, 1886, 6; December 27, 1886, 1; January 9, 1887, 1.

36. Mott, *History of American Magazines*, 4:634.

37. "Bicycle-Making," 5.

38. *Boston Post*, August, 5, 1885, 4.

39. Given all the dangers, diseases, and mishaps Stevens encountered, his minimal ailments and minor injuries are astounding. A twisted knee made riding difficult and painful (2:377), and a particularly bad header produced a debilitating stiffness in his back and shoulders (1:421). On his way through Turkey, he developed a painfully sore throat (2:58). A fever he contracted in Persia (Iran) compelled him to rest and take quinine for two days (2:346, 351).

40. *Columbia Bicycle Catalogue*, 1881, 20.

41. Hawley, "Uses of the Bicycle," 23–24.

42. *Outing*, June 1884, x.

43. *Boston Daily Globe*, August 5, 1884, 1; *Boston Post*, August 5, 1885, 4.

44. Hawley, "Uses of the Bicycle," 24.

45. Hawley, "Uses of the Bicycle," 26.

46. *Columbia Bicycle Catalogue*, 1881, 4.

2. Fanny Bullock Workman

1. "Nun Kun Mountain Group," 39–40. In a seminal article for the *National Geographic Magazine*, Charles E. Fay, the first president of the American Alpine Club, made a similar point: "Probably there is no domain in which the element of pure sport has allied itself to so great an extent with a genuine spirit of scientific research to further human knowledge." Fay, "World's Highest Altitudes and First Ascents," 494.

2. "Nun Kun Mountain Group," 39–40. The few recent accounts of Fanny Workman have tended to slight or belittle her achievements, but contemporaries, unaware of the far greater accomplishments to come, held the Workmans in high regard. Goldie's early praise here was echoed by Charles Fay: "It was in 1898 that Doctor and Mrs. W. H. Workman, of Worcester,

Massachusetts, began the series of excursions that have placed their names among the very highest on the roll of Himalayan explorers." Fay, "World's Highest Altitudes and First Ascents," 504.

3. These addresses, which were published in the June 1893 and June 1896 issues of the *Geographical Journal*, are described in Ellis, *Vertical Margins*, 22, 24–26.

4. *National Cyclopedia of American Biography*, 1:116–17.

5. *New York Times*, June 18, 1881, 5.

6. W. H. Workman Obituary, *New York Times*, October 10, 1937, 53.

7. Fanny Workman, "Bicycle Riding in Germany," 111.

8. Plint, "Workmans," 232.

9. Workman Papers, National Library of Scotland, hereafter cited as NLS.

10. William Workman, letters to T. Fisher Unwin, November 20, 1894, December 29, 1894, and January 14, 1895, NLS.

11. Unwin, *Publishing Unwins*, 42–44.

12. T. Fisher Unwin, Letter to W. H. Workman, March 2, 1895; William Workman, Letter to T. Fisher Unwin, March 10, 1895; March 16, 1905, NLS.

13. Workman and Workman, *In the Ice World*, 98–101.

14. Frison-Roche and Jouty, *History of Mountain Climbing*, 227–28.

15. Workman and Workman, *In the Ice World*, 74.

16. *New York Times*, August 20, 1900, 3. This early interview makes clear that long before her public feud with Annie Peck, Fanny knew about her and the acclaim resulting from her lectures on her conquests of the Matterhorn and other Alpine peaks.

17. Workman and Workman, *Through Town and Jungle* (1904). This final bicycle book was not published until six years after the Workmans' experiences and four years after their first book on climbing in the Himalayas.

18. Mason, *Abode of Snow*, 132–33.

19. Zurbriggen, *From the Alps to the Andes*, 49–105, 148–74, 197–219, 261.

20. Zurbriggen, *From the Alps to the Andes*, 38.

21. Workman and Workman, *In the Ice World*, 140.

22. Workman and Workman, *In the Ice World*, 164–79.

23. Fanny Workman, "Ascent of the Biafo," 523–26. See also Workman and Workman, *In the Ice World*, 164–79.

24. *Scottish Geographical Magazine*, November 1899, 607–8. Apparently the magazine decided that this second article did not warrant publication in full and chose instead to edit it down to a half page of pertinent information.

25. Zurbriggen, *From the Alps to the Andes*, 267. Zurbriggen gives Koser Gunge an elevation of 21,150 feet, which I have amended to 21,000 to keep its elevation consistent with my other citations of it.

26. *Scottish Geographical Magazine*, February 1901, 111.

27. Fanny was awarded fellowship in Royal Scottish Geographical Society on February 29, 1898, and William was elected to the RSGS at a meeting on February 19, 1900.

28. Workman and Workman, *In the Ice World*, 6–9.

29. *Scottish Geographical Magazine*, February 1901, 111.

30. *Geographical Journal*, December 1900, 682.

31. *Geographical Journal*, November 1903, 541–44.

32. William Workman, "Some Obstacles to Himalayan Mountaineering," 504.

33. *Geographical Journal*, March 1905, 245–65. The Workmans provided information for a long article about themselves in the November 1903 issue, but they were not credited as authors.

34. *London Times*, November 22, 1905, 3.

35. *Geographical Journal*, February 1906, 129–30.

36. *Geographical Journal*, November 1906, 505–6. This account implies that clouds compelled William to return and acknowledges that he was fatigued as well. Since a photograph of

Fanny atop Pinnacle Peak, shot from a much lower elevation, shows her with two companion guides, William was probably the photographer.

37. In the earliest reports of her success, Fanny offered this elevation, but later amended it to 23,000 with an error margin of 100 feet either way. Recent computations of its height place it at 22,736. See *Geographical Journal*, November 1907, 108.

38. *Geographical Journal*, November 1907, 108. This brief notice contains a hard-to-believe claim by the Workmans that, at altitudes above twenty-thousand feet, they recorded midafternoon temperatures above 190 degrees Fahrenheit, which held above 140 two hours later.

39. *Bulletin of the American Geographical Society*, March 1908, 231. See also *Scottish Geographical Magazine*, January 1908, 13.

40. Longstaff, *This My Voyage*, 120–28.

41. Longstaff, *This My Voyage*, 102–3.See also *Geographical Journal*, August 1907, 211; September 1907, 331–32. Longstaff claimed that his record was not surpassed until 1930. Longstaff, *This My Voyage*, 104. However, Dr. Alexander Kellas went higher in 1911 when he conquered Panhunri. Frison-Roche and Jouty, *History of Mountain Climbing*, 212.

42. William Workman, "Some Obstacles to Himalayan Mountaineering," 506.

43. *Geographical Journal*, January 1908, 41.

44. *Geographical Journal*, January 1908, 41–42.

45. Fanny Workman, "Highest Camps and Climbs," 257–58.

46. *Geographical Journal*, March 1908, 345.

47. *Geographical Journal*, June 1908, 683–84.

48. Willard, *Woman of the Century*, 563.

49. *New York Times*, January 8, 1898, A2. Willard, *Woman of the Century*, 563; *National Cyclopedia of American Biography*, 15:152. The *National Cyclopedia* entry says that Mount Shasta

was "her first experience in mountain climbing." Almost certainly this should have been "her first experience in mountaineering."

50. *New York Times*, June 14, 1903, 10; *Outing*, December 1904, 623. The Special Collections of the University of Wisconsin (Madison) possesses several brochures containing valuable information about Peck's lectures, including the one on her climbs in the Alps.

51. *New York Times*, January 9, 1898, A2.

52. *New York Times*, January 9, 1898, A2; June 14, 1903, 10.

53. Jordan, "Annie Peck and Popocatepetl," 33–38.

54. "Men and Women of the Outdoor World," 623. See also *New York Times*, January 14, 1903, 10.

55. *New York Times*, July 10, 1904, 11. See also Peck, *Search for the Apex*, 51.

56. *New York Times*, July 10, 1904, SMA11; August 21, 1904, 1; October 9, 1904, SMA3; October 10, 1904, 9; November 27, 1904, SMA5.

57. *New York Times*, October 9, 1904, SMA3.

58. *Outing*, December 1904, 365. *Outing* also ran an article on Peck the year before that announced: "This plucky woman is bound for Bolivia, determined to ascend Mount Sorata, whose height is estimated to be 25,000 feet above sea level. The fact that this feat has before been unsuccessfully attempted does not daunt Miss Peck." *Outing*, August 1903, 623–24.

59. Peck, "Conquest of Huascaran," 357. The actual height of Mount Sorata is 21,490, roughly 190 feet higher than Dr. Tight's calculation.

60. *New York Times*, July 10, 1904, 11.

61. At this time Aconcagua was a crucial reference point for climbers. In 1903, when Dr. Workman began his ascent of Pyramid Peak, he assumed that the current record for elevation belonged to Zurbriggen and Conway for their ascent of Aconcagua and that Aconcagua, at 22,883 feet, was the highest peak in the

Southern Hemisphere. Therefore, when he assessed his elevation on Pyramid Peak to be 23,394, he realized, and subsequently stated, that he had surpassed the elevation of Aconcagua by 500 feet. He believed that anyone hoping to better his new record would have to do so in the Himalayas. See *Geographical Journal*, November 1903, 543. Isserman points out that William's estimated height exceeds the more recently determined elevation of Pyramid Peak. *Fallen Giants*, 53.

62. *New York Times*, August 15, 1908, 1.

63. Peck provides a thorough account of her attempts upon Huascarán in her book *Search for the Apex of America*, 182–354. A good digest of these climbs can be found in Olds, *Women of the Four Winds*, 31–57.

64. *New York Times*, September 8, 1908, 1.

65. Peck, *Search for the Apex*, 339.

66. Peck, "Practical Mountain Climbing," 698; *Search for the Apex*, 339.

67. Peck, "First Ascent of Mount Huascaran," 187.

68. Peck, "Conquest of Huascaran," 356–57.

69. Peck, "Conquest of Huascaran," 363.

70. Peck, "Conquest of Huascaran," 365.

71. *Geographical Journal*, July 1909, 216. See also *Bulletin of the American Geographical Society* 42 (1910): 55.

72. *New York Times*, September 10, 1909, 14.

73. *Bulletin of the American Geographical Society* 42 (1910): 457; *Geographical Journal*, February 1910, 199, 458; *Scientific American*, February 1910, 143.

74. *New York Times*, March 6, 1911, C3.

75. Isserman, *Fallen Giants*, 56; Frison-Roche and Jouty, *History of Mountain Climbing*, 204. In 1934 Hettie Dyhrenfurth accompanied her husband to the 23,861-foot summit of Sia Kangri C.

76. Peck, *Search for the Apex*, 357–58. The *New York Times*

first revealed that Workman's measurement cost her thirteen thousand dollars, March 21, 1911, 8; see also March 26, 1911, C3.

77. *Geographical Journal*, January 1918, 41.

3. Bill Reid

1. Bernstein, *Football*, 6–7.

2. Smith, *Sports and Freedom*, 72–77; Bernstein, *Football*, 9–11.

3. Nelson, *Anatomy of a Game*, 42–50. A convenient listing of the changes implemented by this committee, along with the year in which they were approved, can be found in Baker, *Football: Facts and Figures*, 537–54. Nelson's *Anatomy of a Game* is a more comprehensive history of the many rule changes football has undergone.

4. Bergin, *Game*, 39–40. See also Smith, *Sports and Freedom*, 84–86. Baker identifies several of these "field coaches" and the teams they successfully coached. Baker, *Football*, 170.

5. Baker, *Football*, 271.

6. Bergin, *Game*, 18, 31, 308–10. During these early years Yale and Princeton usually played the Thanksgiving game in New York City. For fuller accounts of the social festivities occasioned by these games, see Pope, *Patriotic Games*, 85–100. See also Smith, *Sports and Freedom*, 78–82; Bernstein, *Football*, 40–48.

7. Smith, *Sports and Freedom*, 128–29. Quoted from a January 26, 1885, memorandum to the faculty of Harvard College. Reprinted in Bergin, *Game*, 22–23.

8. Smith, *Sports and Freedom*, 129–30.

9. Bernstein, *Football*, 36; Smith, *Sports and Freedom*, 90–91.

10. Nelson, *Game* 74–75; Bernstein, *Football*, 54–55.

11. Bernstein, *Football*, 57.

12. The opening chapter of *College Football* offers an extensive recounting of this game. Watterson, *College Football*, 14–17. See also Bernstein, *Football*, 58.

13. Smith, *Sports and Freedom*, 91–92, 130.

14. Bergin, *Game*, 65.

15. Bernstein, *Football*, 58–59.

16. Watterson, *College Football*, 61.

17. Ferrier, *Origin and Development*, 395–99.

18. *Boston Transcript*, July 3, 1902.

19. *Harvard Crimson*, October 6, 1899; October 10, 1899; October 21, 1899; October 22, 1899; October 30, 1899.

20. "Dibblee lost control of himself and has been very bitter toward me on several occasions," Reid wrote in a later assessment of these two players. "And Hollowell I have disliked from the time I entered until now. He is afraid to declare himself and has, so far as I can see, always laid for the views which were worth the most votes." Reid, letter to L. Briggs, February 7, 1904, Harvard University Archives, Cambridge MA, hereafter cited as HUA.

21. *Big-Time Football*, xxi–xxiv.

22. L. Briggs, letter to William T. Reid Jr. January 27, 1904, 3, HUA.

23. Reid, *Debutante's Passion*.

24. Morris, "Harvard Stadium," 836–37.

25. Morris, "Harvard Stadium," 837; *New York Times*, November 22, 1903, 3. The final cost of the stadium, which included an upper colonnade added after World War I, came to $310,000. Stadium clippings, HUA.

26. *New York Times*, December 2, 1905, 7.

27. Reid, letter to L. Briggs, January 2, 1904, 2, HUA.

28. *New York Times*, October 28, 1904, 10.

29. *New York Times*, February 24, 1905, 5.

30. Smith, *Sports and Freedom*, 156. Smith devotes a whole chapter (147–64) to the years of debate that preceded Harvard's hesitant decision to hire a professional coach.

31. Needham, "College Athlete," part 1, June 1905, 118; Lester, *Stagg's University*, 87–88.

32. *Big-Time Football*, 12.

33. *Big-Time Football*, 2–7, 12–14, 26–29.

34. Initially Lewis shared this position with Bertram Waters, but over the course of the season, Lewis evolved into Reid's most trusted ally on his coaching staff.

35. For a fuller account of Lewis's life before and after his association with Harvard football, see Bond, "Strange Career of William Henry Lewis," 39–58.

36. Reid, response to Von Kersburg, July 17, 1948, 8, HUA. Von Kersburg wrote to Reid, who was in Lake Tahoe at the time, and requested that the former coach describe his involvement in the 1905 football crisis. Since Reid believed that his account was to be published, he invested considerable effort in writing this important twenty-three-page document.

37. Reid, letter to L. Briggs, February 7, 1904, 1, HUA.

38. Reid, letter to L. Briggs, January 2, 1904, 10, HUA.

39. Eliot, Reports of the President," 1902–3, 4; 1903–4, 27; 1904–5, 20. The section from Eliot's 1904–5 report, which included his quote about "unnecessary roughness," was republished as "The Evils of Football" in *Harvard Graduates' Magazine*, March 1905, 383–87. The issue of striking another player "with a closed fist" was a bone of contention back in 1883, when the current rules called for a player to be disqualified only after he had used a closed fist a third time. The Harvard Athletic Committee was so offended by this inadequate restriction that it insisted that it be changed or it would not allow the team to play the 1884 season. This dispute originated the "closed fist" and "open hand" distinction.

40. Deming, "Athletics in College Life," 570–71. For *Outlook*'s fall articles on football, see November 18, 1905, 648–50; 662–69; December 7, 1905, 856–57.

41. Needham, "College Athlete," June 1905, 120–23; July 1905, 269.

42. Smith, *Sports and Freedom*, 193–94; Bernstein, *Football*, 79–80; Watterson, *College Football*, 66–69.

43. *Big Time Football*, 194–95; *New York Herald*, October 12, 1905, 1.

44. Watterson, *College Football*, 70.

45. *Big-Time Football*, 195.

46. Smith, *Sports and Freedom*, 88.

47. *Big-Time Football*, 276–82.

48. Reid, response to Von Kersburg, 3–4. See also *Big-Time Football*, 265–66. Reid's letter is reprinted in Smith, *Sports and Freedom*, 195.

49. *New York Times*, November 24, 1905, 7; November 25, 1905, 10.

50. In its account of the game, the *Boston Globe* reported that Burr's nose was broken, but Burr played until late in the fourth quarter, when he left the game due to exhaustion and a rib injury he sustained in an earlier game; his broken nose was not a factor.

51. *Harvard Bulletin*, November 29, 1905, 1.

52. *Harvard Bulletin*, November 29, 1905, 4.

53. Miscellaneous clippings in Special Collections of Nimitz Library, U.S. Naval Academy, Annapolis MD.

54. Edgar Whiting was the linesman, and it is probable that he too was closer to Burr than Dashiell and that he participated in the discussion prior to the umpire's decision. Although both Reid and the Harvard alumni complained that Dashiell was partial to Yale, neither faulted McClung for bias, even though he had been captain and an All-American halfback on Yale's undefeated team of 1891.

55. Apparently, a player who wanted to make a fair catch was supposed to raise his hand as well as "heel" the turf. The "heel" mark was crucial because the hand signal was poorly defined and frequently contested. Reid himself acknowledged, "If the catch was made and the back saw a good chance to run, he did so claiming that he did not signal for a fair catch, but only had his hand up to catch the ball." Reid, response to Von Kersburg, 12.

56. *Boston Globe*, November 26, 1905, 10, 11.

57. *Boston Globe*, November 26, 1905, 11.

58. *Boston Globe*, November 26, 1905, 11. The *Globe*'s account also undermined the credibility of the twenty-five Harvard fans who claimed in the *Bulletin* article that Quill used a closed fist. It reported that Burr was struck "either with the heel of his hand or his elbow (!)."

59. *Big-Time Football*, 313.

60. Reid, response to Von Kersburg, 13. "At the end of the game," Reid wrote, "I told Dashiell he never again would officiate for Harvard and he *never* did."

61. *Boston Globe*, November 27, 1905, 8.

62. Reid, letter to L. Briggs, January 2, 1904, 3, HUA.

63. *Big Time Football*, 163, 253–54, 269.

64. *New York Times*, November 29, 1905, 2; December 5, 1905, 11; December 6, 1905, 8. In "Theodore Roosevelt's Role," Lewis claims that Reid and Roosevelt had a series of meetings over December (723), but does not identify his source for this information. Certainly Reid would have kept Roosevelt fully apprised of the various developments relating to football reform.

65. Reid, response to Von Kersburg, 11.

66. Lewis, "Theodore Roosevelt's Role," 721; Smith, *Sports and Freedom*, 199.

67. During that December the *New York Times* carried at least two articles on Camp's forthright and uncompromising opposition to rule reform. See *New York Times*, December 16, 1905, 9; December, 22, 1905, 7.

68. Reid, response to Von Kersburg, 13.

69. Reid, *Dairy*, vol. 2 (1906), 3–5, HUA.

70. Reid, *Dairy*, vol. 2 (1906), 3–5 (HA); Lewis, "Theodore Roosevelt's Role," 721; Smith, *Sports and Freedom*, 202.

71. *New York Times*, December 27, 1905, 10.

72. Reid, response to Von Kersburg, 16, 19; *New York Times*, January 16, 1906, 8. The fact that the *Times* did not announce this

decision until after the IFA meeting substantiates Reid's assertion (3) that the overseers wanted to impress everyone associated with the rules committees with the gravity of the situation and allow them time to act before news of the decision was made public.

73. John J. Miller's *The Big Scrum: How Teddy Roosevelt Saved Football* was published as this book was being readied for publication. This book's title and text slight the people and administrative units from Harvard that successfully overcame their differences and conspired to achieve rule change. No single individual—neither Roosevelt nor Reid, whose role was equally important—"saved" football during this momentous period of upheaval.

74. Roosevelt, letters to Paul J. Dashiell, December 21, 1905; December 21, 1905; December 30, 1905; January 10, 1906, all in Library of Congress. In his January 10 letter, posted two days before the eventful blending of the two rules committees, Roosevelt wrote Dashiell with an awareness of what was coming and a clear expectation that Dashiell would support Reid: "I earnestly hope that for the purpose of formulating these new rules—and in my judgment there is need of radical innovations among the present rules—you will do all you can to secure the amalgamation of your old rules committee and of this new rules committee."

75. Because Harvard, Yale, and Princeton continued to withhold their support, the new organization remained a fledgling operation for several more years. See Smith, *Sports and Freedom*, 206–8.

76. Reid, response to Von Kersburg, 10–11, 16–17. Ronald Smith presents the fullest accounting of this well-designed game plan for consolidation, which enabled Harvard's influence to supplant that of Yale's. Smith, *Sports and Freedom*, 197–204. See also Lewis, "Theodore Roosevelt's Role," 721–23.

77. Reid, response to Von Kersburg, 6. Many people, including even Camp, realized the necessity of creating open space between the opposing lines of blockers, but Lewis was the one who

suggested that this space be defined in terms of the football. He proposed that the football be situated on the ground so that its ends were parallel to the sidelines and pointed toward the end zones. Blockers then had to position themselves so that no part of their bodies crossed the plane of the closest tip. Since blockers assumed a crouched position supported by a hand on the ground, this hand had to be well back of the tip in order to prevent their heads from intruding on this neutral space.

78. Reid, response to Von Kersburg, 11–12. Critics would later contend that these modifications did not make the game less dangerous. However, Reid's notebook reveals that player injuries dropped from a staggering 145 in 1905 to only 31 in 1906.

79. Reid, response to Von Kersburg, 11–12. For a more complete accounting of these new rules, see Keyes, "New Football," 775–83; also Nelson, *Anatomy of a Game*, 105–26.

80. Reid, response to Von Kersburg, 8–9.

81. Reid, response to Von Kersburg, 14–15.

82. Dashiell clippings in Special Collections of Nimitz Library, U.S. Naval Academy, Annapolis MD.

83. *Big-Game Football*, 326–27. At one point in 1911 Reid wrote to his wife, "I know that you want a masculine man and that it must be a humiliation to you to see others earning so much more." In 1924 she committed suicide. *Big-Time Football*, 327–28.

84. *Twenty-Fifth Report of the Class of 1901*, 501–2.

85. Reid, response to Von Kersburg, 18.

4. May Sutton

1. Sutton, "My Career," 40; "May Bundy's Keen Eyes," *Los Angeles Times*, September 20, 1957, 15. May said in "My Career" that her brother Charles built the court and in the second account that neighbors did. She may have eliminated the neighbors from her original piece in order to downplay the strong English influences on the Suttons' involvement with tennis.

2. There were actually seven siblings in the Sutton family, five daughters and two sons. Adele Sutton, the oldest of the sisters, tried tennis in Plymouth and London but did not play in California.

3. Marion Jones was the first American woman to compete at Wimbledon, in 1900, and she lost in the quarter finals.

4. Sutton, "My Career," 40–41. May's account of these years is riddled with factual errors, which I have modified to accord with the information presented in *Spalding's Lawn Tennis Annual, 1914,* 256.

5. *Pasadena Daily News,* February 12, 1910, 1.

6. California's long, hot, dry summers made grass courts extremely difficult to maintain. During this early period, there were virtually none in Southern California, and its numerous tournaments were all played on concrete, macadam, or dirt courts. When California players traveled out of state to play the National Championships or Wimbledon, they had to allow themselves extra time to adjust their styles of play to the quite different conditions of lawn courts.

7. Sutton, "My Career," 41.

8. Sutton, "Women's Play," 346.

9. Sutton, "Women and Dress," 327.

10. King and Starr, *We Have Come a Long Way,* 18.

11. *New York Times,* November 6, 1909, 2. In 1905 *Harper's Weekly* published an unflattering photo of May, but it shows her in the more practical attire that she favored. *Harper's Weekly,* August 19, 1905, 1197.

12. *New York Times,* June 23, 1904, 7; June 25, 1904, 5.

13. *New York Times,* June 26, 1904, 5.

14. *New York Times,* August 2, 1904, 3.

15. This base of English support helps to explain May's rather odd decision to play Wimbledon three times and to participate in the National Championships only once.

16. *New York Times,* July 9, 1905, 8.

17. Quoted in King and Starr, *We Have Come a Long Way*, 19.

18. *New York Times*, March 19, 1906, 7. The August 19, 1905, issue of *Harper's Weekly* ran a photograph of May Sutton along with a caption stating that she had "never lost a set in a championship match" (1197).

19. *New York Times*, June 9, 1906, 6.

20. *New York Times*, July 4, 1906, 4.

21. *New York Times*, August 19, 1906, 6.

22. *New York Times*, August 25, 1906, 5.

23. *New York Times*, April 7, 1907, SCN20.

24. *New York Times*, April, 27, 1907, 10.

25. *New York Times*, May 4, 1907, 7.

26. *London Times*, July 6, 1907, 9.

27. *Los Angeles Times*, April 22 1906, sec. 2, 1.

28. Carter, *First Lady of Tennis*, 3. Carter reveals that William Hotchkiss was also heavily involved in the planning and development of the Golden Gate Bridge.

29. Klaw, "Queen Mother of Tennis," 18, 20.

30. Wind, "Run, Helen!," 35.

31. *Spalding's Lawn Tennis Annual, 1914*, 256.

32. "House of Hotchkiss," 233. In *Better Tennis*, Hotchkiss mentions this court but does not say when it was built.

33. Quoted in Wind, "Run, Helen!," 38.

34. In an article titled "Inequality of the Sexes in Lawn Tennis," Evelyn Sears identifies these same traits in May and Hotchkiss, but credits only Sutton with the ability to beat men. She claims that May won sets from Niles and McLaughlin (346).

35. Sutton, "Women's Play," 7.

36. *American Lawn Tennis*, October 15, 1907, 295.

37. *American Lawn Tennis*, October 15, 1908, 287.

38. Wightman, *Better Tennis*, 176–77.

39. *San Diego Evening Tribune*, February 23, 1909, 1; *San Diego Sun*, February 23, 1909, 9. See also *American Lawn Tennis*, March 15, 1909, 400–401.

40. *American Lawn Tennis*, July 1, 1909, 83.

41. Klaw, "Queen Mother of Tennis," 24.

42. Quoted in Wind, "Run, Helen!," 43. In this same article a doubles partner of Hazel is quoted as saying, "She's so completely old-fashioned that she thinks people—even deadly rivals on the court—can get along with each other" (31).

43. *New York Times*, June 27, 1909, S2.

44. *New York Times*, January 20, 1909, 12.

45. *Pasadena Daily News*, January 12, 1906, 3; February 5, 1906, 10.

46. *New York Times*, July 8, 1909, 7.

47. *New York Times*, August 5, 1909, 7; August 10, 1909, 7; August 15, 1909, C3; November 6, 1909, 2.

48. A photo from this period shows May playing tennis at a country club in Mexico City. Yeomans, *Southern California Tennis Champions Centennial*, 43. See also *American Lawn Tennis*, May 15, 1909, 31; June 15, 1909, 58. Since Mrs. Ethel Sutton Bruce had been living in Mexico City during the previous year, she probably invited May and her sisters to come there and may have introduced May to Hall.

49. *American Lawn Tennis*, July 15, 1909, 116.

50. *American Lawn Tennis*, March 15, 1910, 390–91.

51. *American Lawn Tennis*, March 15, 1910, 387.

52. *Los Angeles Times*, April 24, 1910, sec. 7, 1. See also *The Ojai*, April, 27, 1910, 1.

53. *American Lawn Tennis*, June 15, 1910, 67.

54. *Los Angeles Times*, May 31, 1910, 18. See also *American Lawn Tennis*, June 15, 1910, 67.

55. Although Sutton never declared these sentiments at the time, she did so the following year. *Los Angeles Times*, July 18, 1911, sec. 3, 1.

56. *American Lawn Tennis*, July 1, 1910, 105.

57. *American Lawn Tennis*, July 15, 1910, 142.

58. Wind, "Run, Helen!," 41.

59. *American Lawn Tennis*, October 15, 1910, 308.

60. *American Lawn Tennis*, October 15, 1910, 308–9.

61. Wind, "Run, Helen!," 41. Contemporary accounts of the match do not mention this break, and one even characterized Sutton's victory as a "clean but desperate win." *American Lawn Tennis* October 15, 1910, 307.

62. Klaw, "Queen Mother of Tennis," 19.

63. Klaw, "Queen Mother of Tennis," 19.

64. *Los Angeles Times*, February 19, 1911, sec. 7, 1.

65. *American Lawn Tennis*, October 15, 1910, 307, 310; December 15, 1910, 367, 370.

66. *New York Times*, June 4, 1911, C7; *American Lawn Tennis*, June 15, 1911, 78.

67. *American Lawn Tennis*, July 1, 1911, 124, 130.

68. *New York Times*, July 1, 1911, 6; October 7, 1911, 14; *American Lawn Tennis* July 1, 1911, 130; July 15, 1911, 130.

69. *American Lawn Tennis*, October 15, 1911, 334.

70. "House of Hotchkiss," 333. Hotchkiss claims that she played Sutton "eight times" since she first won the National Championships in 1909. My research affirms this accounting, and that they played at least twice before this victory. Sutton offers a tally of their meetings, but only for 1911. *American Lawn Tennis*, September 5, 1936, 25.

71. Klaw, "Queen Mother of Tennis," 19; Wind, "Run, Helen!," 43–44. In these two articles Hotchkiss offers slightly different accounts of what she did at this critical juncture, and my account blends them.

72. *American Lawn Tennis*, October 15, 1911, 334.

73. *American Lawn Tennis*, October 15, 1911, 320a.

74. Wightman, *Better Tennis*, 15.

75. *American Lawn Tennis*, October 15, 1911, 321.

76. *New York Times*, September 5, 1911, 12; *American Lawn Tennis*, October 15, 1911, 320, 321.

77. *Pasadena Evening Star*, December 5, 1912, 5. See also *American Lawn Tennis*, January 15, 1913, 415.

78. During Kim Clijsters's comeback victories, most notably at the U.S. Open, the press made much of the fact she was a wife and mother and avoided comment on how unusual she is in women's professional tennis. Prior to this the *New York Times* ran an article revealing that currently there was only one mother among the one hundred top-ranked women tennis players. *New York Times*, June 28, 2007, C20. The demands of competition today are such that few players are even married.

79. *New York Times*, November 26, 1915, 15.

80. *New York Times*, December 12, 1915, 18. May's third child, Dorothy, was born September 1, 1916.

81. *New York Times*, March 11, 1917, S1.

82. *New York Times*, August, 31, 1921, 20; October 23, 1921, 97.

83. *New York Times*, August 19, 1922, 12.

84. *New York Times* August 12, 1925, 22; Engelmann, *Goddess and the American Girl*, 79.

85. *New York Times*, August 25, 1928, 18. See also *American Lawn Tennis*, September 5, 1928, 424.

5. Barney Oldfield

1. Nye, *Hearts of Lions*, 42–53.

2. Cited in Nye, *Hearts of Lions*, 37. The *New York Times* undoubtedly exaggerated Cooper's annual income when it reported that he was making almost $100,000.

3. Nye, *Hearts of Lions*, 37, 60. See also Balf, *Major*, 155–56.

4. Nevins, *Ford*, 1:192–214.

5. *New York Times*, October 5, 1902, 16.

6. DeAngelis, "Ford's '999' and Cooper's 'Arrow,'" 29–30. DeAngelis participated in the restoration of the original 999, and his article is an excellent source of information about both cars. Also Olson, *Young Henry Ford*, 154–56.

7. Quoted in Olson, *Young Henry Ford*, 154.

8. Quoted in Nevins, *Ford*, 1:216.

9. Nolan, *Barney Oldfield*, 35.

10. Oldfield, "Wide Open All the Way," September 19, 1925, 11.

11. Foster, *Castles in the Sand*, 25–26; Bloemker, *500 Miles to Go*, 19. Olds later persuaded Fisher to purchase an estate in Grosse Point. Foster states that Fisher sponsored races involving Oldfield in 1901 but provides inadequate documentation for this suspect information.

12. *Motor Age*, October 9, 1902, 4.

13. *Horseless Age*, October 29, 1902, 485. Oldfield facilitated this anticlimactic appearance by compensating for a failed pump and blowing gas into the pistons from a precarious position behind Cooper.

14. *Motor Age*, October 30, 1902, 7. These suspect reports have been much repeated in subsequent accounts of Oldfield and this important race.

15. Oldfield, "Wide Open All the Way," September 19, 1925, 52.

16. Oldfield, "Wide Open All the Way," September 19, 1925, 54.

17. *Motor Age*, October 30, 1902, 7.

18. Oldfield, "Wide Open All the Way," September 19, 1925, 52.

19. See, for example, *Detroit Free Press*, October 26, 1902; *Automobile Topics*, November 1, 1902. Clippings, Ford, Henry — Racing (Barney Oldfield), Benson Ford Research Center, Dearborn MI.

20. *New York Times*, May 15, 1903, 10; *Motor Age*, November 6, 1902, 16. In his early sketch of Barney Oldfield, Homer George mentioned that Barney received $200 for his Grosse Point victory, and that figure has been much repeated. "Sketch of Barney

Oldfield's Life," 24. The *Times'* report from much closer to the original date is probably more accurate.

21. Oldfield, "Wide Open All the Way," 54. Oldfield, who was careless with details, says that Fisher awarded him and Cooper 25 percent of the receipts for the Dayton race (52), a suspicious figure since neither of the two cars had ever raced. He also misstates that the Toledo race occurred before the Grosse Pointe race. After the big victory at Grosse Pointe, Fisher probably did offer Oldfield and Cooper 25 percent of the Toledo receipts, perhaps more.

22. *Motor Age*, November 6, 1902, 6.

23. *Motor Age*, December 4, 1902, 6; December 11, 1902, 7.

24. *Motor Age*, December 11, 1902, 21. Newspapers were informed that the times were official and approved, but the hastily scheduled events failed to obtain prior authorization. This lack of official approval caused problems with the Diamond Rubber Company, but since its ads were already running, Cooper probably had to settle for a reduced payment.

25. *New York Times*, February 16, 1903, 10.

26. *New York Times*, May 7, 1903, 7. See also *Motor Age*, May 14, 1903, 10.

27. Oldfield, "Wide Open All the Way," September 19, 1925, 54.

28. *New York Times*, May 31, 1903, 15.

29. Oldfield, "Wide Open All the Way," September 19, 1925, 54.

30. *New York Times*, June 21, 1903, 9. See also *Motor Age*, June 25, 1903, 6.

31. *New York Times*, July 26, 1903, 1. See also *Motor Age*, July 30, 1903, 2.

32. *Scientific American*, August 8, 1903, 96.

33. *Motor Age*, July 30, 1903, 2.

34. Oldfield, "Wide Open All the Way," September 19, 1925, 56.

35. *New York Times*, October 30, 1903, 10.

36. *Los Angeles Times*, August 28, 1904, B2.

37. Punnett, *Beach Races*, 21, 25–27. See also *New York Times*, January 29, 1904, 1.

38. Saal and Golias, *Famous but Forgotten*, 50.

39. Camille Jenatzy, for example, was paid a twenty-five-thou-sand-dollar salary and twenty-five-thousand-dollars worth of additional perks for winning the Gordon Bennett Cup in 1903.

40. *New York Times*, March 16, 1904, 1.

41. *New York Times*, April 6, 1904, 7.

42. *Motor Age*, May 14, 1903, 8; *Horseless Age*, May 14, 1903, 4–5.

43. *Motor Age*, December 18, 1902, 6. Although the speed trials at Grosse Pointe conformed to these requirements, Oldfield's records there were not approved because the dates for his trials were not cleared in advance. Board members also viewed Oldfield's car as "a freak."

44. *Boston Globe*, May 27, 1904, 12.

45. Saal and Golias, *Famous but Forgotten*, 57.

46. Unidentified clipping datelined "Columbus, July 4." Oldfield, *Scrapbook*, n.p.; Saal and Golias, *Famous but Forgotten*, 57–59 and 128.

47. *New York Times*, August 29, 1904, 1.

48. *New York Times*, October 30, 1904, 10.

49. *Los Angeles Times*, December 18, 1904, A16. "Auto racing [is] a business, pure and simple," he added years later, "just as a banker makes banking his business." Oldfield, "Wide Open All the Way," September 19, 1925, 61.

50. Oldfield, "Wide Open All the Way," September 25, 1925, 21.

51. *New York Times*, August 9, 1905, 4; August 13, 1905, 9; August 19, 1905, 4.

52. Saal and Golias, *Famous but Forgotten*, 60–61.

53. *Los Angeles Times*, August 23, 1905, sec. 2, 3.

54. *New York Times*, January 17, 1906, 11. The racing scene was so crucial to the show's success that the *Times* ran a special article on its staging. *New York Times*, January 28, 1906, sec. 10, 4. Oldfield and Cooper may have contributed to this staging because they had already devised a scene of their competition for a Detroit auto show. See *Motor Age*, January 18, 1903, 6.

55. *New York Times*, November 20, 1906, 1.

56. Unidentified clipping ca. 1907. Oldfield, *Scrapbook*, n.p.

57. *Los Angeles Times*, June 27, 1905, sec. 2, 3.

58. *Boston Globe*, June 14, 1908, 39; *Los Angeles Times*, May 30, 1909, sec. 5, 12. "I believe the Bullet is the fastest machine in the world and I am proud to say it is of American make," Oldfield once proclaimed. "The American machine is superior even to the French, and is the only kind I would use." *Los Angeles Times*, April 26, 1904, 11.

59. Although many suspected that Oldfield's matches against Cooper and Fisher were arranged, he successfully avoided public accusations until a law suit for fraud was filed against him in Portland in 1907. *New York Times*, July 10, 1907, 5; *Los Angeles Times*, July 5, 1907, sec. 2, 1.

60. Catlin, "54 Bittersweet Years," 394–98.

61. At the time Louis Chevrolet estimated that there were twenty-six road races and forty track races. *New York Times*, January 2, 1910, AU, 2.

62. Doyle, *Ralph De Palma*, 4–6, 22.

63. Doyle, *Ralph De Palma* 28.

64. Doyle, *Ralph De Palma*, 331.

65. *New York Times*, August 8, 1909, S4. See also June 13, 1909, S2.

66. *New York Times*, August 8, 1909, S4; Kimes, *Star and the Laurel*, 124. Kimes says that Oldfield purchased the other 120-horsepower Benz (136), but she does not provide a source for her information.

67. *New York Times*, August 22, 1909, s4. See also September 5, 1909, s4.

68. *New York Times*, October 10, 1909, s4.

69. *New York Times*, November 11, 1909, 10. Fisher immediately contracted Strang and his Fiat to come to Indianapolis for a season-ending time trial, which successfully lowered Oldfield's record for the oval mile. *New York Times*, December 19, 1909, s4.

70. *New York Times*, October 6, 1909, 10. This breakup was probably caused by an abrupt reversal of William Durant's overzealous expansion of General Motors, which forced the company into bankruptcy a year later. Several weeks after Pickens's departure, Hémery took the new Blitzen Benz to the Brooklands car track and set several new records, but intentionally avoided the ones Mephistopheles had previously established.

71. *Los Angeles Times*, December 22, 1909, 17.

72. *New York Times*, October 7, 1909, 10. See also Seneca, *Fairmount Park Motor Races*, 66.

73. Doyle, *Ralph De Palma*, 68–70.

74. As late as April 1910, the *Los Angeles Times* would wrongly report, "De Palma has never met Oldfield in any race." *Los Angeles Times*, April 13, 1910, 17.

75. *Los Angeles Times*, February, 6, 1910, sec. 8, 1.

76. *Los Angeles Times*, March 17, 1910, 17. See also *New York Times*, March 17, 1910, 10. In a separate event Oldfield challenged and bettered the record Hémery had set with the Blitzen Benz at Brooklands.

77. Unidentified clipping dated March 6, 1910. Oldfield, *Scrapbook*, n.p. See also *New York Times*, February 27, 1910, s, 4.

78. *Daytona Daily News*, March 12, 1920. Oldfield, *Scrapbook*, n.p. Although De Palma raced for the Fiat team, E. A. Arnold, a wealthy New Yorker, bought and owned Mephistopheles, and he ordered the car's return.

79. *New Orleans Picayune*, February 7, 1910, 12; Oldfield, *Scrapbook*, n.p.

80. Cancellation of the Daytona race over its unsure purse was so closely connected with verified funding for the Motordrome race that the *Los Angeles Times* ran news of both developments on the same page, clearly implying a close connection between them. *Los Angeles Times*, March 17, 1909, 17.

81. Oldfield, "Wide Open All the Way," September 26, 1925, 130.

82. The *Los Angeles Times* reported contractual disputes over the match between Oldfield and De Palma prior to the race. *Los Angeles Times*, April 12, 1910, sec. 1, 6; April 13, 1910, 17.

83. *New York Times*, April 17, 1910, 8; April 18, 1910, 10.

84. Unidentified clipping dated July 31, 1910. Oldfield, *Scrapbook*, n.p.

85. Knott reports these statements in his much fuller coverage of these incidents. Knott, "Jack Johnson v. Barney Oldfield," 45–47.

86. *New York Times*, October 15, 1910, 12.

87. *New York Times*, October 20, 1910, 14.

88. *New York Times*, November 3, 1910, 10.

89. Quoted in Nolan, *Barney Oldfield*, 105.

90. *Los Angeles Times*, December 18, 1910, sec. 7, 4.

91. *New York Times*, April 13, 1910, 12.

92. Doyle, *Ralph De Palma*, 116.

93. *Los Angeles Times*, November 20, 1910, sec. 7, 1.

94. Catlin, "54 Bittersweet Years," 401–2.

95. *New York Times*, April 14, 1912, C12.

96. Nolan, *Barney Oldfield*, 112–24. See also Doyle, *Ralph De Palma*, 127–30.

97. *Los Angeles Times*, February 1, 1914, sec. 8, 1; February 6, 1914, sec. 2, 1.

98. De Palma also probably realized that Earl Cooper had opted for a slower, steadier speed against Oldfield during his victory over him at Corona.

99. Nolan, *Barney Oldfield*, 134. See also Doyle, *Ralph De Palma*, 139.

100. De Paolo, *Wall Smacker*, 72–73. De Paolo went on to win the 1925 Indianapolis 500 and did so using Firestone tires.

Epilogue

1. Fountain, *Sportswriter*, 95.

2. John Dizikes has cogently observed: "Once play became sport, Americans played a double game: the game within the rules and the game against the rules." Dizikes, *Sportsmen and Gamesmen*, 311.

Bibliography

Introduction and Epilogue

Dizikes, John. *Sportsmen and Gamesmen*. Boston: Houghton Mifflin, 1981.

Evensen, Bruce J. *When Dempsey Fought Tunney: Heroes, Hokum, and Storytelling in the Jazz Age*. Knoxville: University of Tennessee Press, 1996.

Fountain, Charles. *Sportswriter: The Life and Times of Grantland Rice*. New York: Oxford University Press, 1993.

Guttmann, Allen. *From Ritual to Record: The Nature of Modern Sports*. New York: Columbia University Press, 1978.

Hardy, Stephen. "'Adopted by All the Leading Clubs': Sporting Goods and the Shaping of Leisure." In *Sport in America: From Wicked Amusement to National Obsession*, edited by David K. Wiggins, 133–50. Champaign IL: Human Kinetics, 1995.

Inabinett, Mark. *Grantland Rice and His Heroes: The Sportswriter as Mythmaker in the 1920s*. Knoxville: University of Tennessee Press, 1994.

Levine, Peter. *A. G. Spalding and the Rise of Baseball*. New York: Oxford University Press, 1985.

Mott, Frank Luther. *A History of American Magazines*. 5 vols. Cambridge MA: Harvard University Press, 1938–68.

Oriard, Michael. *King Football: Sport and Spectacle in the Golden Age of Radio and Newsreels, Movies and Magazines, the*

Weekly & the Daily Press. Chapel Hill: University of North Carolina Press, 2001.

Pope, S. W. *Patriotic Games: Sporting Traditions in the American Imagination, 1876–1926.* New York: Oxford University Press, 1997.

Rader, Benjamin G. *American Sports: From the Age of Folk Games to the Age of Televised Sports.* 6th ed. Englewood Cliffs NJ: Prentice Hall, 2008.

1. Tom Stevens

Bagg, Lyman [Karl Kron]. *10,000 Miles on a Bicycle.* New York: Karl Kron, 1887.

"Bicycle-Making: Where and How Bicycles Are Made." *Frank Leslie's Popular Monthly,* 1882. Reprinted in *Wheelmen,* Winter 1972, 2.

Columbia Bicycle Catalogue. Pope Manufacturing Co. 1881. Special Collections, University of Delaware Library, Newark.

Geist, Roland. "The American Bicycle Hall of Fame." *Wheelmen,* November 1971, 7–8.

Goddard, Stephen B. *Colonel Albert Pope and His American Dream Machines.* Jefferson NC: McFarland, 2000.

Hawley, C. E. "Uses of the Bicycle." *Wheelman,* October 1882, 23–24.

Herlihy, David V. *Bicycle: The History.* New Haven: Yale University Press, 2004.

"History on the Go!" *Connecticut Historical Society Workbook,* 6th ser., 17–18.

Howland, Edward. "A Bicycle Era." *Harper's Monthly,* July 1881, 282.

Leonard, Irving. "Colonel Albert A. Pope and the Bicycle," *Wheelmen* Summer, 1971, 7–8.

———. *First across America.* Privately printed, 1969.

———. "Thomas Stevens and the League of American Wheelmen." *Wheelmen,* March 1978, 8–10.

"Outing's Portrait Gallery: Thomas Stevens." *Outing*, May 1887, 183–85.

Pope, Albert. "Colonel Albert A. Pope's Response." *Wheelman*, October 1882, 69–70.

Pratt, Charles E. *The American Bicycler: A Manual.* Boston: Houghton, Osgood, 1879.

———. "The Wheel around the Hub Tour." *Scribner's*, February 1880, 481–99.

Smith, Robert A. *A Social History of the Bicycle: Its Early Life and Times in America.* New York: American Heritage, 1972.

Stevens, Thomas. *Around the World on a Bicycle.* 2 vols.. New York: Scribner's, 1887–88. Reprint, Mechanicsburg PA: Stackpole Press, 2001.

———. "Bicycling in the Far West." *Outing and the Wheelman*, September 1884, 463–64.

Wells, S. Michael. "Sunrise in America: The Wheel around the Hub Tour." *Wheelmen*, May 1995, 3–9.

2. Fanny Bullock Workman

Briggs, Berta N. "Peck, Annie Smith. In *Notable American Women, 1607–1950*, edited by Edward T. James, 3:40–42. Cambridge MA: Harvard University Press, 1971.

Ellis, Reuben. *Vertical Margins: Mountaineering and the Landscapes of Neoimperialism.* Madison: University of Wisconsin Press, 2001.

Farrar, J. P. "Fanny Bullock Workman." *Alpine Journal* 37 (1925): 180–82.

Fay, Charles E. "The World's Highest Altitudes and First Ascents." *National Geographic*, June 1909, 494–504.

Frison-Roche, Roger, and Sylvain Jouty. *A History of Mountain Climbing.* Paris: Flammarion, 1996.

Isserman, Maurice. *Fallen Giants: A History of Himalayan Mountaineering from the Age of Empire to the Age of Extremes.* New Haven CT: Yale University Press, 2008.

Jordan, Elizabeth. "Annie Peck and Popocatepetl." *New Yorker*, October 3, 1936, 33–38.

Kraig, Beth. "Workman, Fanny Bullock." In *American National Biography*, edited by John A. Garraty and Mark Carnes, 23:877–79. New York: Oxford University Press, 1999.

Knowlton, Elizabeth. "Workman, Fanny Bullock." In *Notable American Women, 1607–1950*, edited by Edward T. James, 3:672–74. Cambridge MA: Harvard University Press, 1971.

Longstaff, Thomas George. *This My Voyage*. New York: Scribners', 1950.

Mason, Kenneth. *Abode of Snow: A History of Himalayan Exploration and Mountaineering*. London: Rupert Hart-Davis, 1955.

"Men and Women of the Outdoor World." *Outing*, August 1903, 623–24.

Middleton, Dorothy. *Victorian Lady Travelers*. London: Routledge & Kegan Paul, 1965.

Miller, Luree. *On Top of the World: Five Women Explorers in Tibet*. Frome, England: Paddington, 1976.

"Nun Kun Mountain Group and Its Glaciers—Discussion." *Geographical Journal*, January 1908, 39–40.

Olds, Elizabeth Fagg. *Women of the Four Winds*. Boston: Houghton Mifflin, 1985.

Peck, Annie. "Climbing Mount Sorata." *Appalachia*, May 1906, 95–110.

———. "The Conquest of Huascaran." *Bulletin of the American Geographical Society* 41 (June 1909): 355–65.

———. "The First Ascent of Huascaran." *Harper's Monthly*, January 1909, 173–87.

———. *Flying over South America*. Boston: Houghton Mifflin, 1932.

———. *Industrial and Commercial South America*. 1922. Rev. ed. New York: Crowell, 1927.

———. "Practical Mountain Climbing." *Outing*, September 1901, 695–700.

———. *A Search for the Apex of America: High Climbing in Peru and Bolivia, including the Conquest of Huascaran, with Some Observations on the Country and People Below.* New York: Dodd, Mead, 1911.

———. "A Woman's Conquest of the Andes." *American Review of Reviews*, October 1908), 488–89.

Plint, Michael. "Workmans: Travelers Extraordinary." *Alpine Journal* 97 (1992–93), 231–37.

Polk, Milbry. *Women of Discovery: A Celebration of Intrepid Women Who Explored the World.* New York: C. Potter, 2001.

Stefoff, Rebecca. *Women of the World.* New York: Oxford University Press, 1992.

Tinling, Marion. *Women into the Unknown: A Sourcebook on Women Explorers and Travelers.* New York: Greenwood, 1989.

Unwin, Philip. *The Publishing Unwins.* London: Heinemann, 1972.

Willard, Frances E. *Woman of the Century: Fourteen Hundred-Seventy Biographical Sketches accompanied by Portraits of Leading American Women in All Walks of Life.* Buffalo NY: Moulton, 1893.

Workman, Fanny Bullock. "The Altitude of Mount Huascaran." *Geographical Journal*, April 1910, 458–59.

———. "Amid the Snows of Baltistan." *Scottish Geographical Magazine*, February 1901, 74–86.

———. "Ascent of the Biafo Glacier and Hispar Pass; Two Pioneer Ascents in the Karakoram." *Scottish Geographical Magazine*, October 1899, 523–26.

———. "Bicycle Riding in Germany." *Outing*, November 1892, 110–11.

———. "First Exploration of the Hoh Lumba and Sosbon Glaciers:

Two Pioneer Ascents in the Himalayas." *Geographical Journal*, February 1906, 129–41.

———. "Highest Camps and Climbs." *Appalachia*, April 1907, 257–59.

———. "Mountaineering in the Himalayas." *English Illustrated Magazine*, August 1902, 443–52.

———. "Record Mountain Climbing in the Himalayas." *Appleton's Magazine*, October 1907), 387–98.

Workman, Fanny Bullock, and W. H. Workman. *Algerian Memories: A Bicycle Tour over the Atlas to the Sahara*. London: T. F. Unwin, 1895.

———. *Ice-Bound Heights of the Mustagh: An Account of Two Seasons of Pioneer Exploration and High Climbing in the Baltistan Himalaya*. London: A. Constable, 1908.

———. *In the Ice World of Himalaya: Among the Peaks and Passes of Ladakh, Nubra, and Baltistan*. London: T. F. Unwin, 1900.

———. *Peaks and Glaciers of Nun Kun: A Record of Pioneer Exploration and Mountaineering in the Punjab Himalayas*. London: A. Constable, 1909.

———. *Sketches Awheel in Fin de Siècle Iberia*. London: T. F. Unwin, 1897.

———. *Through Town and Jungle: Fourteen Thousand Miles A-Wheel among the Temples and People of the Indian Plain*. London: T. F. Unwin, 1904.

Workman, William Hunter. "An Exploration of the Nun Kun Mountain Group and Its Glaciers." *Geographical Journal*, January 1908, 12–39.

———. "From Srinagar to the Sources of the Chogo Lungma Glacier." *Geographical Journal*, March 1905, 245–65.

———. "The Question of Mr. Johnson's High Camp." *Geographical Journal*, June 1908, 683–84.

———. "Some Obstacles to Himalayan Mountaineering and the

History of a Record Ascent." *Alpine Journal*, August 1905, 489–506.

———. "Tent Life in the Himalayas." *Outing*, April 1901, 68–73.

Zurbriggen, Matthias. *From the Alps to the Andes: Being the Autobiography of a Mountain Guide*. London: T. Fisher Unwin, 1989.

3. Bill Reid

Anderson, Lars. *Carlisle vs. Army: Jim Thorp, Dwight Eisenhower, Pop Warner and the Forgotten Story of Football's Greatest Battle*. New York: Random House, 2007.

Baker, Louis Henry. *Football: Facts and Figures*. New York: Rinehart, 1945.

Bergin, Thomas G. *The Game: The Harvard-Yale Rivalry, 1875–1983*. New Haven CT: Yale University Press, 1984.

Bernstein, Mark F. *Football: The Ivy League Origins of an American Obsession*. Philadelphia: University of Pennsylvania Press, 2001.

Big Time Football at Harvard, 1905: The Diary of Coach Bill Reid. Edited by Ronald Smith. Urbana: University of Illinois Press, 1994.

Bingham, William T. "Story of the Appointment of the Officials for the Harvard-Yale Game, 1905." HUA.

Blanchard, John Adams. *The H Book of Harvard Athletics, 1852-1922*. Cambridge: Harvard Varsity Club, 1923.

Bond, Gregory. "The Strange Career of William Henry Lewis." In *Out of the Shadows: A Biographical History of African American Athletes*, edited by David K. Wiggins, 39–57. Fayettevillle: University of Arkansas Press, 2006.

Deming, Clarence. "Athletics in College Life: The Money Power in College Athletics." *Outlook*, July 1905, 569–72.

Eliot, Charles W. "The Evils of Football." *Harvard Graduates' Magazine*, March 1905, 383–87.

———. *Reports of the President of Harvard College.* 1902–3, 1903–4, 1904–5. HUA.

Ferrier, William Warren. *The Origin and Development of the University of California.* Berkeley CA: Sather Gate Book Shop, 1930.

Jenkins, Sally. *The Real All Americans: The Team That Changed a Game, a People, a Nation.* New York: Doubleday, 2007.

Keyes, Homer Eaton. "The New Football: Origin and Meaning of the Revised Rules." *Outlook,* November 1906, 775–83.

Lester, Robin. *Stagg's University: The Rise, Decline, and Fall of Big-Time Football at Chicago.* Urbana: University of Illinois Press, 1995.

Lewis, Guy. "Theodore Roosevelt's Role in the 1905 Football Controversy." *Research Quarterly* 90 (December 1969): 717–24.

Miller, John J. *The Big Scrum: How Teddy Roosevelt Saved Football.* New York: Harper, 2011.

Moore, John Hammond. "Football's Ugly Decades, 1893–1913." *Smithsonian Journal of History* 1–2 (Fall 1967): 49–68.

Morris, George P. "The Harvard Stadium." *Outlook,* August 1904, 836–37.

Needham, Henry Beach. "The College Athlete." *McClure's,* June 1905, 115–28; July 1905, 260–73.

Nelson, David M. *The Anatomy of a Game: Football, the Rules, and the Men Who Made Them.* Newark: University of Delaware Press, 1994.

Pope, S. W. *Patriotic Games: Sporting Traditions in the American Imagination, 1876–1926.* New York: Oxford University Press, 1997.

Reid, William T., Jr. *A Debutante's Passion—A Coach's Erotica: Love Letters of a Harvard Man and a Boston Elite.* Edited by Ronald A. Smith. Lemont PA: Eifrig, 2009.

———. *Diary, 1906.* HUA.

———. Response to Letter from H. E. Von Kersburg, July 17, 1948. HUA.

Smith, Ronald. *Sports and Freedom: The Rise of Big-Time College Athletics*. New York: Oxford University Press, 1988.

Watterson, John Sayle. *College Football: History, Spectacle, Controversy*. Baltimore: Johns Hopkins University Press, 2000.

4. May Sutton

Carter, Tom. *First Lady of Tennis: Hazel Hotchkiss Wightman*. Berkeley CA: Creative Arts, 2000.

Chambers, Lambert. *Tennis for Ladies*. London: Methuen, 1910.

Collins, Bud, and Zander Hollander. *Bud Collins' Modern Encyclopedia of Tennis*. Detroit: Gale, 1994.

Engelmann, Larry. *The Goddess and the American Girl: The Story of Suzanne Lenglen and Helen Wills*. New York: Oxford University Press, 1988.

"House of Hotchkiss." *American Lawn Tennis*, October 15, 1911, 3.

King, Billie Jean, and Cynthia Starr. *We Have Come a Long Way: The Story of Women's Tennis*. New York: McGraw-Hill, 1988.

Klaw, Barbara. "Queen Mother of Tennis: An Interview with Hazel Hotchkiss Wightman." *American Heritage*, August 1975, 16–24, 82–86.

Little, Alan. *May Sutton: The First Overseas Wimbledon Champion*. Sherborne, Dorset, England: Remons, 1984.

"May Bundy's Keen Eyes." *Los Angeles Times*, September 20, 1957, 15.

Phelps, Frank V., "Wightman, Hazel Hotchkiss." In *American National Biography*, edited by John A. Garraty and Mark Carnes, 23:357–59. New York: Oxford University Press, 1999.

Sears, Evelyn. "Inequality of the Sexes in Lawn Tennis." *American Lawn Tennis*, November 15, 1911, 346.

Spalding Official Lawn Tennis Annual, 1914. New York: American Sports Publishing, 1914.

Sutton, May. "The California Game Comes East: How Tennis in

the East and Abroad Looked to a Young Girl from the Golden State." In *Fifty Years of Lawn Tennis in the United States,* 110–13. New York, 1931.

———. "My Career as a Lawn Tennis Player." *American Lawn Tennis,* May 15, 1912, 40–41.

———. "Women and Dress." *Harper's Bazaar,* May 1910, 327.

———. "Women's Play and How to Improve it." *American Lawn Tennis* (November 15, 1911, 346.

Wightman, Hazel Hotchkiss. *Better Tennis.* Boston: Houghton, Mifflin, 1933.

Wind, Herbert Warren. "Run, Helen!" *New Yorker,* August 30, 1952, 31–49.

Yeomans, Patricia Henry. *Southern California Tennis Champions Centennial, 1887–1987: Documents & Anecdotes.* Los Angeles: Southern California Committee for the Olympic Games, 1987.

5. Barney Oldfield

Bailey, L. Scott. "The Great Barney Oldfield." *Antique Automobile,* June 1960, 181–84.

Balf, Todd. *Major: A Black Athlete, a White Era, and the Fight to Be the World's Fastest Human.* New York: Crown, 2008.

Bloemker, Al. *500 Miles to Go: The Story of the Indianapolis Speedway.* New York: Coward-McCann, 1961.

Carey, Charles W., Jr. "Oldfield, Barney." In *American National Biography,* edited by John A. Garraty and Mark Carnes, 16:671–72. New York: Oxford University Press, 1999.

Catlin, Russ. "54 Bittersweet Years." *Automobile Quarterly* 20, no. 4 (1982): 394–417.

DeAngelis, George. "Ford's '999' and Cooper's 'Arrow.'" *Antique Automobile,* November–December 1993, 29–37.

De Paolo, Peter. *Wall Smacker: The Saga of the Speedway.* Cleveland: Thompson, 1935.

Doyle, Gary D. *Ralph De Palma: Gentleman Champion*. Oceanside CA: Golden Age Books, 2005.

Foster, Mark S. *Castles in the Sand: The Life and Times of Carl Graham Fisher*. Gainesville: University Press of Florida, 2000.

Fox, Stephen R. *Big Leagues: Professional Baseball, Football, and Basketball in National Memory*. Lincoln: University of Nebraska Press, 1998.

George, Homer C. "Sketch of Barney Oldfield's Life." Introduction to *Barney Oldfield's Book for the Motorist*. Boston: Small, Maynard, 1919.

Howell, Mark. "'You Know Me!' Barney Oldfield and the Creation of a Legend." *Auto Historical Review*, Summer 2000, 26–30.

Kimes, Beverly Rae. *The Star and the Laurel: The Centennial History of Daimler, Mercedes and Benz*. Montvale NJ: Mercedes Benz, 1986.

———. "Vanderbilt Cup Races, 1904–1910." *Automobile Quarterly* 6, no. 2 (1967): 184–99.

Knott, Rick. "The Jack Johnson v. Barney Oldfield Match Race of 1920: What Race Says about America." *Afro-Americans in New York Life and History* 29 (January 2005): 39–53.

Ludvigsen, Karl. *The Incredible Blitzen Benz*. Deerfield IL: Dalton Watson, 2006.

Messer-Kruse, Timothy. "You Know Me: Barney Oldfield." *Timeline*, May–June, 2002, 2–21.

Nevins, Alan. *Ford: The Times, the Man, the Company*. 3 vols. New York: Scribners, 1954.

Nolan, William. *Barney Oldfield: The Life and Times of America's Legendary Speed King*. New York: Putnam, 1961.

Nye, Peter. *Hearts of Lions*. New York: Norton, 1988.

Oldfield, Barney. Scrapbook. LA84 Foundation, Los Angeles.

Oldfield, Barney, with William F. Sturm. "Wide Open All the Way." *Saturday Evening Post*, September 19, 1925, 10–11, 50–61; September 26, 1925, 20–21, 129–37.

Olson, Sidney. *Young Henry Ford: A Picture History of the First Forty Years*. Detroit: Wayne State University Press, 1963.

Punnett, Dick. *Beach Races: Daytona before NASCAR*. Gainesville: University of Florida Press, 2008.

Riggs, L. Spencer. "Carl Fisher." *Automobile Quarterly* 35, no. 2 (1996): 67–81.

Saal, Thomas E., and Bernard J. Golias. *Famous but Forgotten: The Story of Alexander Winton, Automotive Pioneer and Industrialist*. Twinsburg OH: Golias, 1997.

Seneca, Michael J. *The Fairmount Park Motor Races, 1908–1911*. Jefferson NC: McFarland, 2003.

Index

Lightning Source UK Ltd.
Milton Keynes UK
UKHW010959200320
360651UK00012B/46